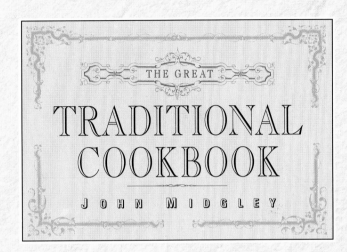

THE GREAT

TRADITIONAL COOKBOOK

JOHN MIDGLEY

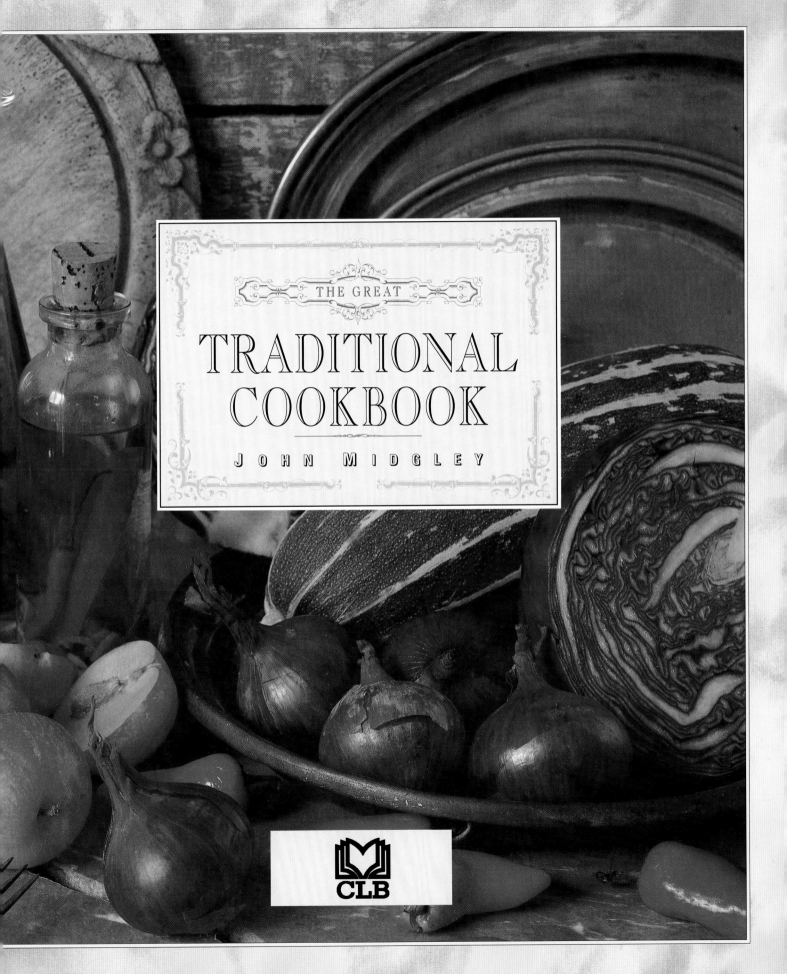

THE GREAT

TRADITIONAL
COOKBOOK

JOHN MIDGLEY

CLB

The Great Traditional Cookbook

Designed and created by
THE BRIDGEWATER BOOK COMPANY LTD

Designers Peter Bridgewater/Tony Norman
Editor Veronica Sperling
Managing Editor Anna Clarkson
Photography Trevor Wood
Food preparation and styling Jon Higgins
Page make-up Chris Lanaway

CLB 4166
This edition published 1995 by Colour Library Books
© 1995 Colour Library Books Ltd, Godalming, Surrey
All rights reserved
Colour separations by Sussex Repro, England
Printed and bound in Singapore

ISBN 1-85833-345-8

AUTHOR'S ACKNOWLEDGEMENTS

I would like to thank *Peter Bridgewater* and *Anna Clarkson* of *Bridgewater Book Company*,
who commissioned me to write this book, and who were responsible for designing
it so beautifully; *Trevor Wood*, for his splendid photography; *Jon Higgins*;
and last but not least *Sue Midgley*, who has helped me enormously
at all stages and with all aspects of the book.

The dates quoted for the Victorian cookbooks used vary according to the editions cited.

CONTENTS

PART ONE
BREADS & ROLLS

PART TWO
SANDWICHES & SAVOURIES

PART THREE
SOUPS

PART FOUR
SALADS, VEGETABLES
& ACCOMPANIMENTS

CONTENTS

CONTENTS

PART NINE
CAKES & DESSERTS

PART TEN
SAVOURY PRESERVES AND PICKLES

PART ELEVEN
DRINKS

My main concern has been to present Victorian food as appealingly as possible. Taken 'raw', some Victorian recipes do not quite match up to current culinary expectations, and since so much has changed in respect of ingredients and their packaging, kitchen equipment and methods of preparation, many – though by no means all – Victorian recipes need some degree of translation to render them usable, relevant and attractive, from one hundred and fifty-eight to ninety-four years after they were first written down. (I am using as my point of reference the dates of Queen Victoria's reign: 1837–1901.)

In selecting, re-interpreting and adapting Victorian and other traditional recipes I have taken fully into account some of the issues that concern us most such as healthy eating, quickness and ease of preparation, use of supermarket ingredients, and so on.

Of course, I would not wish to suggest that the Victorians did not care for their health, nor that they always ate more complicated food than we do, nor even that Victorian cooks had much more time and resources to lavish on its preparation. Although the affluent were leisured, the great middle-class Victorian cookery writers such as Isabella Beeton and Eliza Acton, and even professional chefs such as Alexis Soyer and Charles Francatelli often placed great importance on simplicity and 'economy'. It is just that the culinary circumstances have changed beyond recognition, and so has the available knowledge about what constitutes a healthy diet.

Finally, I readily admit that by allowing my own tastes and preferences to hold sway, this is inevitably a very personal book. Occasionally I have created entirely new recipes that remain true to the spirit if not to the letter of Victorian food. Above all, this is a cookery book, meant to be cooked from. I hope and trust that you will enjoy using it in your kitchen again and again.

VICTORIAN DOMESTIC ENVIRONMENT AND EATING HABITS

A yawning gulf separated the domestic circumstances, diet and eating habits of the class of Victorians to whom Francatelli addressed his *A Plain Cookery Book for the Working Classes*, and Soyer, his *A Shilling Cookery for the People*, and those more privileged subjects at the other end of the socio-economic spectrum.

For the former, meat was a rare luxury, and stodge, whether in the form of potatoes and bread or grain and pulse-based gruels, batters, puddings and pies filled the stomach. Moreover, the poorer classes had to cope with the widespread and shocking adulteration of their food, and the appallingly unhygenic conditions that prevailed in the cookshops frequented by labourers and factory-workers. Since the domestic kitchens of the poor lacked ovens, much of their food was eaten at these establishments or had to be bought ready-cooked, and anything that required baking or roasting was sent to communal ovens or to the baker's.

By contrast, the rich enjoyed superb, abundant produce. Theirs was a rich diversity of meat from livestock, game, and fowl, not forgetting fish, dairy products, and fruits and vegetables, all from the estate and therefore unadulterated by devious middle men. The grandest households employed several chefs – often French, who were attracted to Britain by the high wages on offer – and each with different responsibilities, as well as an army of servants.

Further down the scale, even the more prosperous middle class households employed some though not all of the domestic staff mentioned in Mrs Beeton's *Book of Household Management*, namely: 'Housekeeper, Cook, Kitchen-Maid, Butler, Footman, Coachman, Valet, Upper and Under Housemaids, Lady's Maid, Maid-Of-All-Work, Laundry-Maid, Nurse and Nurse-Maid, Monthly, Wet and Sick Nurses, Etc. Etc.' A more typical standard household might have kept a cook, an upper and a lower housemaid, a nanny or nursery maid, and a manservant.

The authors whose published recipes I have consulted most are Mrs Beeton, Eliza Acton, Christina Johnstone (under the pseudonym of Meg Dods), Alexis Soyer and Charles Elmé Francatelli. I am struck by the profoundly comforting nature of the food, and by the authors' thrifty good sense and obvious enjoyment of everything edible.

Routine middle-class dinner parties consisted of up to thirty dishes, many more when a more formal occasion demanded greater ostentation. For example, a December bill of fare chosen at random from Mrs Beeton's *Book of Household Management suggests a succession of twenty-six dishes for a 'dinner for 18 persons', arranged as follows:*

FIRST COURSE
Two soups and two fish 'removes'
Two further fish dishes
~
'ENTREES'
Three meat dishes
One fish curry
~
SECOND COURSE
One haunch (mutton)
One savoury pie (game)
One stew (beef)
Two fowl (boiled turkey, and roast goose)
~
THIRD COURSE
Two fowl (pheasants, and ducks), and two sweet 'removes'
Eight further sweets, including cake, pudding, pies, creams, and jellies
~
This, to be followed by 'dessert and ices'!

Part One
BREADS & ROLLS

*T*HE WONDERFUL aroma of freshly baked bread is always a delight, and although there has never before been such a wide choice of different breads of excellent quality to buy, home-baking more than repays the very small effort invested.

Victorian recipes for breads and rolls include traditional golden saffron buns, soft milk bread for children, and the unlikely-sounding rice bread rolls, which contrast a nice crust with a light, moist middle; some, such as potato bread were popular in part for their excellent keeping qualities, while others, such as the attractively freckled 'Irish brade breached' and yeastless soda bread originated in remote, traditional areas.

The labour of kneading, which many find pleasurably sensual and relaxing, can be removed by machine-kneading. It is important that the dough should be worked until smooth and elastic. It should also be remembered that the oven times and temperatures specified are never infallible, as ovens vary in their efficiency, the flour type and quality, ambient temperature and humidity all conspire to affect the outcome. The old-fashioned test that you can rely upon is the knock on the base; bread is ready when it sounds hollow.

MORNING ROLLS

Glazed Geneva rolls, with the warm
flavour and colour of saffron.

HOT ROLLS As soon as the rolls come from the baker's, they should be put into the oven, which, in the early part of the morning, is sure not to be very hot; and the rolls must not be buttered until wanted. When they are quite hot, divide them lengthwise into three; put some thin flakes of good butter between the slices, press the rolls together, and put them in the oven for a minute or two, but not longer, or the butter would oil; take them out of the oven, spread the butter equally over, divide the rolls in half, and put them on to a very hot clean dish, and send them instantly to table.

ISABELLA BEETON, *Book of Household Management (1861)*

GENEVA ROLLS

☞ ½ tsp saffron strands
4 tbs hand-hot water
900 g/2 lb plain flour
75 g/3 oz butter, diced
pinch of salt
4 tsp easy-blend dried yeast
560 ml/1 pint milk, warmed
2 eggs at room temperature, beaten
1 beaten egg yolk or milk, to glaze

Dissolve the saffron in the water and allow it to stand until the water takes on the strong colour. In a large warm bowl mix together the flour, butter, salt and yeast. Gradually add the saffron water and approximately three-quarters of the warmed milk and knead either by hand or machine until the dough is smooth and elastic. Cover the bowl with a cloth and leave in a warm place to rise for approximately 1 hour or until the dough has risen appreciably. Reheat the remaining milk and stir half of it into the eggs. Add the mixture to the dough and knead again briefly. (If the dough seems dryish at this point the remaining milk may be added, otherwise it may be retained to glaze the rolls.) Leave in a warm place for another 45 minutes. Preheat the oven to 230°C/450°F/gas mark 8. Grease a baking tray and divide the dough into 16-18 small rolls, glaze and bake for 15 minutes. Reduce the heat to 220°C/425°F/gas mark 7 and bake for about 5 minutes longer or until the rolls are golden brown and sound hollow when tapped on the base.

ELIZA ACTON'S RECIPE

Break down into very small crumbs three ounces of butter with two pounds of flour; add a little salt, and set the sponge with a large tablespoonful of solid yeast, mixed with a pint of new milk, and a table-spoonful or more of strong saffron water; let it rise a full hour, then stir to a couple of well-beaten eggs as much hot milk as will render them lukewarm, and wet the rolls with them to a light, lithe dough; leave it from half to three-quarters of an hour longer, mould it into small rolls, brush them with beaten yolk of egg, and bake them from twenty minutes to half an hour.

ELIZA ACTON, *Modern Cookery for Private Families (1855)*

DELICIOUS BREADS

POTATO BREAD

Eliza Acton recommends this as an 'excellent bread, which will remain moist much longer than wheaten bread made as usual'. Indeed it does! This makes one large loaf.

☞ *225 g / 8 oz potatoes*
350 g / 12 oz strong white bread flour
110 g / 4 oz flour
2 tsp easy-blend dried yeast
1 tsp salt
25 g / 1 oz butter, diced
225 ml / 8 fl oz warm water

Peel and boil the potatoes until cooked. Drain, and when sufficiently cool to handle, grate coarsely. In a warm bowl mix the flours, yeast, salt and butter together with the grated potato. Gradually add the water and knead either by hand or machine until the dough is smooth and elastic. Cover the bowl with a clean cloth and leave to rise in a warm place for approximately 1 hour or until the dough has risen to an appreciable degree.

Grease a 450 g / 1 lb loaf tin. Knead the dough again briefly then fit it into the tin and leave in a warm place for about 45 minutes longer. Preheat the oven to 230°C / 450°F / gas mark 8. Bake for 15 minutes then reduce the heat to 220°C / 425°F / gas mark 7 and bake for about 20 minutes longer or until the loaf is golden brown and sounds hollow when tapped on the base.

MILK BREAD

This makes a nice soft loaf with a good storage life which endeared it to the Victorians. Milk bread is perfect for tea-time or indeed for breakfast and children's parties.

☞ *450 g / 1 lb strong white bread flour*
1 egg
50 g / 2 oz butter at room temperature
2 tsp easy-blend dried yeast
¼ tsp salt
1 tsp sugar
225 ml / 8 fl oz warm milk
beaten egg or milk, to glaze

Sift the flour into a large warm bowl and add the egg, butter, yeast, salt and sugar. Gradually mix in the milk – the full quantity may not always be necessary – and knead either by hand or machine until the dough is smooth and elastic. Cover the bowl with a clean cloth and leave to rise somewhere warm until the dough has risen a fair amount or for approximately 1 hour.

Grease a 450 g / 1 lb loaf tin. Knead the dough again briefly, then fit it into the tin. Leave somewhere warm for about 45 minutes longer. Preheat the oven to 230°C / 450°F / gas mark 8. Glaze the top and bake for 15 minutes, then reduce the heat to 220°C / 425°F / gas mark 7 and bake for about 20 minutes longer or until the loaf is golden brown and sounds hollow when tapped on the base.

Both milk and potato bread have a sumptuous, soft texture and have good keeping qualities, if only it were possible to resist eating the loaves at once.

LIGHT CRUSTY ROLLS

These little rolls made with a dough mixing rice, milk and flour are exceptionally light in texture.

RICE BREAD ROLLS

These bread rolls are based on Mrs Beeton's original recipe. Their texture is light and moist but with a good crust, and they taste really delicious.

☞ 110 g / 4 oz long-grain rice, rinsed and drained
450 ml / 15 fl oz milk
575 g / 1¼ lb strong white bread flour
2 tsp salt
25 g / 1 oz butter, diced
3 tsp easy-blend dried yeast
300 ml / 10 fl oz water

Boil the rice in the milk until tender. Do not drain but allow to cool a little and then add to the flour, salt, butter and yeast. Gradually add the water and knead either by hand or machine until the dough is smooth and elastic. Cover the bowl with a clean cloth and leave to rise in a warm place for approximately 1 hour or until the dough has risen appreciably. Knead the dough again briefly and divide into 10 rolls which should be placed on a large, greased baking tray and left in a warm place for about 45 minutes longer. Preheat the oven to 230°C/450°F/gas mark 8. Bake for 15 minutes then reduce the heat to 220°C/425°F/ gas mark 7 and bake for 5–10 minutes longer or until the rolls are golden brown and sound hollow when tapped on the base.

MOTTLED IRISH LOAF

*This 'breached' or spotted bread is especially
good lightly toasted and served with afternoon tea.*

IRISH 'BRADE BREACHED'

According to Mrs Dods, whose recipe I have adapted here, this mottled loaf was the holiday-cake of Munster. 'Breached' is the Irish word for spotted or freckled, which describes the pleasant appearance of the bread perfectly. It is especially good when lightly toasted and served with afternoon tea.

☞ *225 g/8 oz strong white bread flour*
1 tsp easy-blend dried yeast
50 g/2 oz butter, melted
140 ml/5 fl oz warm water, plus extra if necessary
50 g/2 oz sugar
50 g/2 oz currants
50 g/2 oz raisins
25 g/1 oz flaked almonds, chopped
12 g/½ oz candied orange peel, diced

In a warm bowl mix together the flour, yeast and butter. Gradually add the water and knead either by hand or machine until the dough is smooth and elastic. Cover the bowl with a clean cloth and leave to rise in a warm place for approximately 1 hour or until the dough has risen appreciably. Grease a 450 g/1 lb loaf tin. Knead the dough again briefly, add the remaining ingredients, fit into the loaf tin, cover with a cloth, and leave to rise in a warm place for 40 minutes. Preheat the oven to 200°C/400°F/gas mark 6. Bake for 30-40 minutes or until well risen, golden brown and hollow-sounding when tapped on the base.

By scoring a cross on top of soda bread before baking, the loaf can simply be pulled into four chunks.

SODA BREAD

⋎

Soda bread was common in many remote parts both of England and Ireland, where it was often very difficult to obtain a regular supply of good yeast. Dried fruits, candied peel, or spices may also be added.

☞ *225 g/8 oz plain white flour*
1 tsp bicarbonate of soda
1 tsp salt
1 tsp sugar
½ tsp cream of tartar
170 ml/6 fl oz buttermilk

Preheat the oven to 200°C/400°F/gas mark 6. Mix all the dry ingredients together with the buttermilk, and knead either by hand or machine until a soft dough is formed. Roll the dough into a round shape about 3 cm/1¼ inches high, score a cross on the top of the loaf, place on a greased oven sheet and bake for 25–30 minutes or until the bread is well risen and golden and sounds hollow when tapped on the base.

Originally an Irish bread, there are many varieties of soda bread. Some are wonderfully sweetened with dried fruits or honey. This is based on Mrs Beeton's recipe.

ON SODA

Soda was called the mineral alkali, because it was originally dug up out of the ground in Africa and other countries; this state of carbonate of soda is called natron. But carbonate of soda is likewise procured from the combustion of marine plants, or such as grow on the sea-shore. Pure carbonate of soda is employed for making effervescent draughts, with lemon-juice, citric acid, or tartaric acid...A small pinch of carbonate of soda will give an extraordinary lightness to puff pastes; and, introduced into the teapot, will extract the full strength of the tea.

ISABELLA BEETON, *Book of Household Management (1861)*

Part Two
SANDWICHES & SAVOURIES

*T*HE SANDWICH was 'invented' by John Montagu, the fourth Earl of Sandwich (1718–1792); a notorious gambler, he once dedicated an entire day and night to the pursuit of his vice, and ordered meat between slices of bread to be brought to him to avoid the interruption of retiring to table. By Victorian times sandwiches had become more elaborate and ubiquitous. The origin of the old chestnut of the appalling institutional sandwich can perhaps be traced back to the Victorian cookery writer Christina Jane Johnstone who, writing under the pseudonym of Meg Dods (a character created by her friend Sir Walter Scott) observed in her *Cook and Housewife's Manual:*

'...these are a convenient and economical, but, at the same time, a rather suspicious order of culinary preparations, especially in hotels and public gardens: they are therefore getting into disrepute.'

Acknowledging that a snack is as good or indifferent as its ingredients, how they are treated, and how freshly made, I have chosen a wide variety of recipes. These range from neat, dainty delicacies such as correct cucumber sandwiches and popular potted savouries through more substantial, traditional toasts.

DAINTY SANDWICHES FOR TEA-TIME

CUCUMBER SANDWICHES

A 1909 RECIPE

INGREDIENTS – *1 large cucumber, creamed butter, white or brown bread, salad-oil, lemon-juice or vinegar, salt and pepper.*

METHOD – *Peel the cucumber, slice it thinly, season liberally with salt, drain on a hair sieve for 1 hour, and dry thoroughly. Now put it into a basin and sprinkle with pepper, salad-oil, lemon-juice, or vinegar, liberally or otherwise according to taste. Have ready some thin slices of bread and butter, stamp out some rounds of suitable size, place slices of cucumber between 2 rounds of bread, and press the parts well together. Dish slightly overlapping each other in a circle on a folded serviette, and serve garnished with parsley.*

From a later edition of Mrs Beeton's *Book of Household Management.*

SPICY EGG & ANCHOVY SANDWICHES

Here is a recipe for a spicy egg and anchovy sandwich spread that is equally delicious on hot buttered toast. This makes 12 small sandwiches.

☞ *2 eggs*
6 small anchovy fillets, coarsely chopped
2–3 sprigs parsley, finely chopped
3 tbs grated Cheddar cheese
¼ tsp curry powder
dash of Worcestershire sauce
⅛ tsp cayenne (optional)
1 tbs butter, at room temperature
6 slices brown bread, buttered
sprigs of watercress, to garnish

Boil the eggs until the whites are solid but the yolks retain moist centres; unrefrigerated eggs brought to the boil in a pan of cold water should be perfectly cooked in just 4 minutes. Let the eggs cool down, peel them, scoop out the yolks and discard the whites.

With a mortar and pestle, pound the anchovy fillets, egg yolks, parsley, cheese, curry powder, Worcestershire sauce, cayenne (if using) and butter. When smooth and sticky spread the paste on half of the buttered bread slices, cover with the rest of the bread and cut each sandwich into 4 triangles. Arrange daintily on a clean, crisply starched napkin and serve garnished with sprigs of watercress for a delicious treat in the afternoon.

Quintessentially British cucumber
sandwiches, without which the proper
tea-time spread would be incomplete!

*Francatelli's hefty sole fillet
sandwiches — a complete meal in themselves,
and rather a luxury at today's prices.*

SANDWICHES OF FILLETS OF SOLES

Simmer the fillets of soles in a saucepan with a little clarified butter, pepper, salt, and lemon-juice; when done, put them in press between two dishes, and afterwards divide each fillet into four scollops; trim, and put them into a basin with a little mignionette-pepper, salt, oil, and vinegar. Some small oval rolls must be ordered for this purpose; after the tops are cut off, and the crumb removed, first strew the bottom of each roll with small salad, then place a scollop of sole upon this, add a little Mayonnaise sauce, then strew some small salad on the surface, cover with the tops, and dish them up.

NOTE – *Sandwiches of lobster or salmon are prepared in a similar manner.*

 ## BADMINTON SANDWICH

Cut some square pieces from a half-quartern loaf of stale bread, barely a quarter of an inch thick; toast these of a light colour, and immediately on their being taken from the fire, let them be split or divided with a sharp knife, the inner or untoasted sides must be spread with anchovy butter, and over this place closely some fillets of anchovies; cover the whole with the other piece of toast previously spread with anchovy butter, press down the sandwich with a knife, and after having cut the preparation into small oblong shapes, dish them up and serve.

SUMMER SANDWICH

Between thin slices of white or brown bread and butter, place some very thin slices of any of the following kinds of meats: ham, tongue, boiled or roast beef, roast mutton, poultry or game, season with pepper and salt and a little mustard; strew some mustard and cress, small salad, or, if preferred, some finely-shred lettuce, over the meat; press the sandwich together with the blade of a knife, cut it into small oblong shapes, which, having dished up neatly, send to table.

All three recipes are from Charles Elmé Francatelli's The Modern Cook *(1896)*

TASTY CHEESY BITES

A tempting cheesy array, Meg Dods's pastry ramekins on the left, and her cheese (and ham) sandwiches to the right.

These are a convenient and economical, but, at the same time, a rather suspicious order of culinary preparations, especially in hotels and public gardens: they are therefore getting into disrepute. Sandwiches may be made of ham or tongue, sliced, grated or scraped; of German or common pork sausage, cold salted rump, anchovies, shrimps, sprats, potted cheese, or hard yolks of eggs and Parmesan or Cheshire cheese pounded with butter; forcemeat, and potted meat of various kinds, cold poultry, with whatever seasonings, as mustard, curry-powder, &c. &c. are most suitable to the meat of which the sandwich is made. The only particular directions that can be given, are, to have them fresh-made, and to cut the bread in neat even slices, and not too large nor thick.

The remarks on sandwiches, and the three ensuing cheese recipes are all taken from
Meg Dods's Cook and Housewife's Manual (1829)

A CHEESE SANDWICH

Take two parts of grated Parmesan or Cheshire cheese, one of butter, and a small proportion of made-mustard; pound them in a mortar; cover slices of bread with a little of this, and over it lay thin slices of ham, or any cured meat; cover with another slice of bread, press them together, and cut this into mouthfulls, that they may be lifted with a fork.

PASTRY RAMEKINS

Take any bits of puff-paste that remain from covering pies, tarts &c. and roll them lightly out. Sprinkle grated cheese over them of any rich highly-flavoured kind. Fold the paste up in three, or only double it, but sprinkle it repeatedly with grated cheese. Shape the ramekins with a paste-runner to any shape, and bake or serve them hot on a napkin or as relishes. This is almost *Brioches au fromage*.

TO POT CHEESE

Cut down half a pound of good sound mellow Stilton, with two ounces of fresh butter; add a little mace and made mustard. Beat this well in a mortar, and pressing it close in a potting-pan, cover with clarified butter if to be kept long. Curry or anchovy powder, cayenne or pepper, may all be added to the cheese.

The Victorians loved potted foods which kept well for long periods under a seal of clarified butter. This is a splendid bowl of potted shrimps.

POTTED SHRIMPS OR PRAWNS

Let the fish be quite freshly boiled, shell them quickly, and just before they are put into the mortar, chop them a little with a very sharp knife; pound them perfectly with a small quantity of fresh butter, mace, and cayenne.

Shrimps (unshelled), 2 quarts; butter, 2 to 4 oz.; mace, 1 small saltspoonful; cayenne, $\frac{1}{3}$ as much.

ELIZA ACTON, *Modern Cookery for Private Families (1855)*

ALEXIS SOYER'S OYSTERS ON TOAST

Open twelve very large oysters, put them in a pan with their liquor, a quarter of a teaspoonful of pepper, a wineglass of milk, two cloves, and a small piece of mace, if handy; boil a few minutes until set, mix one ounce of butter with half an ounce of flour, put it, in small pieces, in the pan, stir around; when near boiling pour over the toast, and serve. A little sugar and the juice of a lemon, is a great improvement.

From *A Shilling Cookery for the People (1859)*

POTTED MUSHROOMS

Prepare either small flaps or buttons with great nicety, without wetting them, and wipe the former very dry...Stew them quite tender, with the same proportion of butter as the mushrooms au beurre, but increase a little the quantity of spice; when they are done turn them into a large dish, spread them over one end of it, and raise it two or three inches that they may be well drained from the butter. As soon as they are quite cold, press them very closely into potting-pans; pour lukewarm clarified butter thickly over them, and store them in a cool dry place.

ELIZA ACTON, *Modern Cookery for Private Families (1855)*

Spicy potted chicken makes a delicious spread for hot toast.

Truss a pheasant as for boiling, and braise it with 1lb. of ham, in some well-seasoned wine mirepoix; when done, drain them upon a dish, strain their liquor into a stewpan, and when divested of all the grease, boil it down to glaze. Meanwhile, chop and pound all the meat from the pheasant with the ham, and add to these 6oz. of clarified fresh butter, a ragout-spoonful of good sauce, and the glaze; season with Cayenne pepper, a little nutmeg and salt, and pound the whole thoroughly, and rub this preparation through a fine wire-sieve on to a dish. Next, fill some small round or oval earthenware potting-pans with this preparation, smooth the surface over with a spoon dipped in water, place them in a covered stewpan, and submit them to the action of steam for about half an hour. The potted pheasant must then be allowed to cool; then, with the bowl of a spoon, press down the meat in the pots, wipe them clean, and run a little clarified butter over the surface.

NOTE – All kinds of game should be potted in the above manner, and will then keep fresh-flavoured for months. For those who approve of it, more spice and aromatic herbs may be added; but it should be observed, that an immoderate use of these impairs the flavour of the game.

CHARLES ELMÉ FRANCATELLI, *The Modern Cook, (1896)*

WELL-PRESERVED SANDWICH SPREADS

POTTED CHICKEN

225 g/8 oz cold roast chicken, shredded
75 g/3 oz smoked ham
50 g/2 oz butter
1 tsp salt
¼ tsp cayenne
½ tsp ground mace
¼ nutmeg, grated
clarified butter, to cover

Combine all the ingredients in a food processor until a smooth paste forms. Fill potting-pots or ramekins with the mixture and cover with a 5 mm/¼ inch layer of clarified butter. The original recipe recommends that, if intended for storage, the potted chicken should have a bladder tied over it; the squeamish may prefer to use cling-film and store in the fridge which is just as effective! The pots should be removed from the fridge and allowed to reach room temperature. Spread on hot toast or use as a sandwich filling.

POTTED HAM

I.

<u>INGREDIENTS</u> – To 4 lbs. of lean ham allow 1 lb. of fat, 2 teaspoonfuls of pounded mace, ½ nutmeg grated, rather more than ½ teaspoonful of cayenne, clarified lard.

<u>MODE</u> – Mince the ham, fat and lean together in the above proportion, and pound it well in a mortar, seasoning it with cayenne pepper, pounded mace, and nutmeg; put the mixture into a deep baking-dish, and bake for ½ hour; then press it well into a stone jar, fill up the jar with clarified lard, cover it closely, and paste over it a piece of thick paper. If well seasoned, it will keep a long time in winter, and will be found very convenient for sandwiches, &c.

<u>TIME</u> – ½ hour   Seasonable at any time.

II.

<u>INGREDIENTS</u> – To 2 lbs. of lean ham allow ½ lb. of fat, 1 teaspoonful of pounded mace, ½ teaspoonful of pounded allspice, ½ nutmeg, pepper to taste, clarified butter.

<u>MODE</u> – Cut some slices from the remains of a cold ham, mince them small, and to every 2 lbs. of lean, allow the above proportion of fat. Pound the ham in a mortar to a fine paste, with the fat, gradually add the seasoning and spices, and be very particular that all the ingredients are well mixed and the spices well pounded. Press the mixture into potting-pots, pour over clarified butter, and keep it in a cool place.

ISABELLA BEETON, *Book of Household Management (1861)*

GOURMET MUSHROOMS ON TOAST

Rich, delicious croûte aux champignons, a gourmet treat.

MUSHROOM-TOAST
OR
CROÛTE AUX CHAMPIGNONS

*C*ut the stems closely from a quart or more of small just-opened mushrooms; peel them, and take out the gills. Dissolve from two to three ounces of fresh butter in a well-tinned saucepan or stewpan, put in the mushrooms, strew over them a quarter of a teaspoonful of pounded mace mixed with a little cayenne, and let them stew over a gentle fire from ten to fifteen minutes; toss or stir them often during the time; then add a small dessertspoonful of flour, and shake the pan round until it is lightly browned. Next pour in, by slow degrees, half a pint of gravy or of good beef broth; and when the mushrooms have stewed softly in this for a couple of minutes, throw in a little salt, and a squeeze of lemon-juice, and pour them on to a crust, cut about an inch and a quarter thick, from the under part of a moderate-sized loaf, and fried in good butter a light brown, after having been first slightly hollowed in the inside. New milk, or thin cream, may be used with very good effect instead of the gravy; but a few strips of lemon-rind, and a small portion of nutmeg and mushroom-catsup should then be added to the sauce. The bread may be buttered and grilled over a gentle fire instead of being fried, and is better so.

Small mushrooms, 4 to 5 half pints; butter, 3 to 4 oz.; mace, mixed with a little cayenne, $^{1}/_{4}$ teaspoonful: stewed softly for 10 to 15 minutes. Flour, 1 small dessertspoonful: 3 to 5 minutes. Gravy or broth, $^{1}/_{2}$ pint: 2 minutes. Little salt and lemon-juice.

ELIZA ACTON, *Modern Cookery for Private Families (1855)*

TOASTED CHEESE

WELSH RABBIT

> oast a round of bread from a quartern loaf; put about four ounces of cheese into a small saucepan or pipkin with a teaspoonful of mustard, a little pepper and salt, and a wineglass of ale; break the cheese small, set it on the fire, and stir until it is melted, then pour over the toast, and serve quickly.
>
> 2ND – Toast a round of bread, and place on it two pieces of cheese, single Gloucester, a quarter of an inch thick; place it before the fire, and as the cheese melts, spread it over the bread with a knife, also a little cayenne and mustard.
>
> 3RD – Take a penny French roll, cut off a thin slice from one end, and take out some of the crumb and place it in the oven. Melt the cheese as above, and pour it into the roll. It is very good for a journey, or a sportsman, and can be eaten cold.
>
> 4TH, OR IRISH RABBIT – Toast a round of bread; chop up four ounces of cheese, a small piece of butter, one gherkin, some mustard, pepper, and salt, until it is quite a paste; spread it over the toast, and place them in the oven for five minutes, and serve hot.
>
> ALEXIS SOYER, *A Shilling Cookery for the People (1859)*

Many's the long night I've dreamed of cheese — toasted, mostly.

ROBERT LOUIS STEVENSON,
Treasure Island

MEG DODS'S
WELSH GALLIMAUFRY

Mix well in a mortar, cheese with butter, mustard, wine, flavoured vinegar, or any ingredient admired, ad libitum.

Soyer's 'Irish Rabbit' a savoury which includes sliced gherkins and mustard.

TOASTED CHEESE This academic, histrionic, and poetical preparation has produced a great deal of discussion in its day. The Welsh Rabbit, (by the way, we are inclined to think with a learned friend, that the true reading is Welsh Rare Bit,) has ever been a favourite morsel with those gentlemen who think a second supper fairly worth the other three regularly-administered meals of the day. The twenty-eighth maxim of O'DOHERTY is wholly dedicated to this tasteful subject, and his culinary opinions are worthy of profound attention. "It is the cant of the day," quoth Sir MORGAN "to say that a Welsh Rabbit is heavy eating. I know this, – but did I ever feel it in my own case? – Certainly not. I like it best in the genuine Welsh way, however; - that is, the toasted bread buttered on both sides profusely, then a layer of cold roast beef, with mustard and horserelish, then on the top of all a superstratum of Cheshire thoroughly saturated while in the process of toasting with *cwrw*, or, in its absence, porter – genuine porter – black-pepper, and eschalot-vinegar. I peril myself upon the assertion that this is not a heavy supper for a man who has been busy all day till dinner in reading, writing, walking, or riding, – or who has occupied himself between dinner and supper in the discussion of a bottle or two of sound wine, or any equivalent, and who proposes to swallow at least three tumblers of something hot ere he resigns himself to the embrace of Somnus. With these provisoes, I recommend toasted cheese for supper.

MEG DODS, *Cook and Housewife's Manual (1829)*

Part Three
SOUPS

*S*OUP IS as old as the hills, and was originally a miserable broth bulked out by bread, a habit that still flourishes in our more affluent times, whether in the form of bread-dunking or in the more sophisticated guise of croûtons. 'Soup' derives from the late Latin verb *suppare* (to soak) which, like the English noun 'sop' (food soaked in a liquid) probably has Germanic roots.

I have tailored my selection to suit current tastes and offer you a range of excellent healthy potages that are either deeply traditional or specifically Victorian, such as Mrs B's own cucumber soup (which, incidentally, tastes just fine made with chicken stock).

These are soups for all seasons. Hence a lovely springtime soup bursting with fresh green vegetables, and a maigre potato soup originally taken in Lent (no beef, mutton or veal stock here, just the vegetable kind); summer's warmth is encapsulated in a wonderful fresh tomato soup that would be the envy of Messrs Heinz, and my hot, spicy version of the Victorian favourite mulligatawny, through its heat, will be found most cooling in hot weather; a trio of thicker, warming soups of peas, beans and lentils are ideal for cooler nights as the days draw in; my spiced parsnip soup puts to perfect use a root vegetable whose flavour is enhanced by winter frosts.

A POTAGE OF LOVE-APPLES

FRESH TOMATO SOUP

This delicious tomato soup, with a touch of cayenne for an authentic Victorian flavour is far superior to any canned version. It is best made in summer, when tomatoes are cheap and plentiful. For the fresh tomato base see the recipe for Shaker Stewed Tomatoes page 80. This makes enough for eight people.

☞ *2.5 kg / 5 lb ripe tomatoes*
110 ml / 4 fl oz olive oil or 110 g / 4 oz butter
3 tbs tomato purée
1 tbs sugar
1.7 litres / 3 pints chicken or vegetable stock, preferably home-made
¼ tsp cayenne (optional)
salt and freshly milled black pepper
110 ml / 4 fl oz single cream
small bunch of fresh parsley, basil or chives, finely chopped

Make the tomato base exactly as indicated in the recipe for Shaker Stewed Tomatoes, adding the tomato purée and sugar when reduced, but stew the tomatoes for just 1 hour. Add the stock, and cayenne (if using), and bring to a simmer. Cover the pan and simmer for 15–20 minutes. Allow to cool, then liquidize until completely smooth. Check the seasoning and briefly reheat the soup without boiling. Ladle into soup bowls, adding a swirl of cream to each. Sprinkle with the chosen herb and eat immediately with buttered slices of good wholemeal bread.

THE TOMATO, OR LOVE-APPLE

This vegetable is a native of Mexico and South America, but is also found in the East Indies, where it is supposed to have been introduced by the Spaniards. In this country it is much more cultivated than it formerly was; and the more the community becomes acquainted with the many agreeable forms in which the fruit can be prepared, the more widely will its cultivation be extended. For ketchup, soups, and sauces, it is equally applicable, and the unripe fruit makes one of the best pickles.

ISABELLA BEETON, *Book of Household Management (1861)*

There is nothing quite like a tomato soup made with glowing red, fresh tomatoes; enrich and colour it with a swirl of cream and plenty of chopped fresh green herbs for a truly magical dish.

HEARTY, WARMING POTATO SOUPS

*Floury potatoes, aromatic celeriac and mildly
pungent leeks combine wonderfully in this earthy,
smooth-textured soup, the traditional precursor of
later chefs' innovations such as vichyssoise.*

GERMAN POTATO SOUP

*This traditional and very tasty soup is perfect for a
light lunch or supper. Originally a Lenten dish, it can be
made either with plain water or with vegetable stock,
which is more flavoursome. Accompanied by a salad, this
delightful, creamy-coloured soup serves four.*

☞ *25 g/ 1 oz butter*
675 g/ 1½ lb baking potatoes, peeled and diced
675 g/ 1½ lb peeled, diced celeriac (root celery)
*(or the equivalent weight in celery and additional
potatoes, chopped)*
1 large onion, peeled and chopped
white part of 1 leek, peeled and chopped
salt and freshly milled black pepper
1.8 litres/ 3¼ pints vegetable stock
small bunch of fresh chives, snipped

Heat the butter in a large pan until foaming. Add the vegetables and sauté for a few minutes. Season, add the stock and bring to the boil. Cover, reduce the heat and simmer for 30 minutes. Allow the mixture to cool a little, then liquidize and return to the pan. Check the seasoning and reheat without boiling. Sprinkle with the chives, ladle into soup bowls and eat straight away. NOTE: Be sure to use floury potato varieties such as Catriona, Maris Piper, Pentland, Golden Wonder or any large baking potatoes.

ENGLISH POTATO SOUP

Mash to a smooth paste three pounds of good mealy potatoes, which have been steamed, or boiled very dry; mix with them by degrees, two quarts of boiling broth, pass the soup through a strainer, set it again on the fire, add pepper and salt, and let it boil for five minutes. Take off entirely the black scum that will rise upon it, and serve it very hot with fried or toasted bread. Where the flavour is approved, two ounces of onions minced and fried a light brown, may be added to the soup, and stewed in it for ten minutes before it is sent to table.

ELIZA ACTON, *Modern Cookery for Private Families (1855)*

43

SPRINGTIME SOUP

This and other similar soups were very popular with the Victorians. The soup should be delicate yet tasty; it is certainly healthy. For a more gutsy, rustic Italian version, add some shredded cabbage, replace the French beans and asparagus with cooked borlotti or cannellini beans, and sprinkle with freshly grated Parmesan (or drizzle with extra virgin olive oil). Accompanied by crusty bread, this is ample for four people.

☞ *2 carrots, peeled and finely diced*
2 small turnips, peeled and finely diced
2 celery sticks,
2 small leeks, cleaned, halved vertically and sliced
25 g/1 oz butter
1³/₄ litres/3 pints chicken or vegetable stock
salt and freshly milled black pepper
1 lettuce heart, coarsely shredded
large handful of baby spinach leaves, coarsely shredded
75 g/3 oz cooked French beans, coarsely chopped
50 g/2 oz cooked asparagus tips
handful of fresh parsley, chopped

Sauté the carrots, turnips, celery and leeks in the butter for 3–4 minutes. Add the stock, bring to the boil, then reduce the heat and season. Cover and simmer for 25 minutes (skimming off some of the fat). Add the lettuce and spinach. Return to a simmer and cook for 5 minutes longer. When ready, check the seasoning and add the cooked beans and asparagus. Ladle into soup bowls, garnish with parsley and eat straight away.

The essence of spring is encapsulated in this deliciously delicate soup, in which the vivid green colour of tender new vegetables shines through.

A RICH FRENCH CUCUMBER SOUP

Mrs Beeton's 'finest French recipe' for cucumber soup is subtly flavoured with sour-tasting sorrel and the popular Gallic herb chervil, and enriched with egg yolks and cream.

MRS BEETON'S CUCUMBER SOUP
(FINEST FRENCH RECIPE)

INGREDIENTS — *1 large cucumber, a piece of butter the size of a walnut, a little chervil and sorrel cut in large pieces, salt and pepper to taste, the yolks of 2 eggs, 1 gill of cream, 1 quart of medium stock.*

MODE — Pare the cucumber, quarter it, and take out the seeds; cut it in thin slices, put these on a plate with a little salt, to draw the water from them; drain, and put them in your stewpan, with the butter. When they are warmed through, without being browned, pour the stock on them. Add the sorrel, chervil, and seasoning, and boil for 40 minutes. Mix the well-beaten yolks of the eggs with the cream, which add at the moment of serving. Sufficient for 4.

THE CUCUMBER — The antiquity of this fruit is very great. In the sacred writings we find that the people of Israel regretted it, whilst sojourning in the desert; and at the present time, the cucumber, and other fruits of its class, form a large portion of the food of the Egyptian people. By the Eastern nations generally, as well as by the Greeks and Romans, it was greatly esteemed. Like the melon, it was originally brought from Asia by the Romans, and in the late 14th century it was common in England, although, in the time of the wars of "the Roses," it seems no longer to have been cultivated. It is a cold food, and of difficult digestion when eaten raw. As a preserved sweetmeat, however, it is esteemed one of the most agreeable.

ISABELLA BEETON, *Book of Household Management (1861)*

Cook's Tip

This recipe makes a delicious soup. If you don't have chervil and sorrel to hand, a little finely chopped spinach and parsley may be substituted. If you prefer a smooth soup, pour the contents of the pan into a food processor and liquidize, then return to the pan, reheat, and stir in the egg yolk and cream mixture just before serving. One quart is equivalent to 1.1 litres/2 pints, and a gill is equal to 110 ml/4 fl oz.

A very thick, hearty cold-weather
soup, which makes a meal in itself.

YELLOW SPLIT PEA AND BACON SOUP

*My delicious rib-sticking interpretation of this very traditional English soup
is perfect for cold winter days. Accompanied with croûtons or thick buttered
chunks of home-made bread this makes enough for four people.*

☞ *225 g / 8 oz yellow split peas*
225 g / 8 oz potatoes, peeled and diced
3 tbs extra virgin olive oil
75 g / 3 oz lean bacon, rinded and diced
1 onion, finely chopped
1 celery stick, finely diced
1 large carrot, scrubbed and finely diced
1.4 litres / 2½ pints chicken or vegetable stock
salt and freshly milled black pepper
2–3 tsp dried mint, crumbled

Put the peas and the potatoes into a large pan with a good covering of salted water and bring to the boil. Simmer until both have softened and the mixture is quite dry (about 20 minutes). Set aside.

Heat the oil in another large pan and fry the bacon until just browned, then add the onion, celery and carrot. Reduce the heat to medium and stir-fry for about 6 minutes. Add the peas and potatoes, and the stock. Bring to the boil, then reduce the heat. Cover the pan and simmer for 1 hour, stirring occasionally. Season and simmer for 10 minutes longer. The peas and potatoes should have melted into the soup which will have become quite thick. Sprinkle with mint and serve immediately.

A similar soup can be made with green split peas. Mint is traditionally included in split pea soup not only as a seasoning but also to remedy the somewhat gaseous side-effects of the peas!

Take a quart of yellow split-peas, wash them several times in water, drain them, and put them into a small stockpot with half a pound of raw ham, two heads of celery, one carrot, and an onion with four cloves stuck in it, add three quarts of common broth, let the soup boil, skim it well, and then set it by the side of the stove-fire to boil gently for about three hours. The peas having then become entirely dissolved, pass them through a tammy-cloth with the aid of two wooden spoons, spread the tammy-cloth over a large dish, pour the purée, or part thereof, into the hollow thus formed; then let two persons take hold firmly of each end of the tammy-cloth with the left hand, so as carefully to secure the purée against flowing over; then, with the right hand, they should work the edge of the spoon, the bowls being back to back, in the cloth, in regular time and with some force until the whole of the purée is rubbed through: it will be, however, necessary to scrape off with the back of a large knife any portion that may adhere to the cloth. When this is done, hasten to remove the purée from the dish into a soup-pot of adequate size; add a large ladleful of consommé, carefully stirring the purée on the stove-fire until it begins to boil, then remove it to the side of the stove, to continue gently boiling until it has clarified itself by throwing up all the froth, which should be removed as it rises to the surface. Ascertain whether the seasoning be palatable, and send to table with some dried and sifted mint in a plate; and in another plate serve some Condé crusts.

CHARLES ELMÉ FRANCATELLI, *The Modern Cook (1896)*

EARTHY PULSES FOR EASY NOURISHING SOUPS

RED KIDNEY BEAN SOUP

LENTIL SOUP

This convenient but delicious soup can be made with canned kidney beans, and tastes even better when reheated the next day; dried beans must be soaked overnight, then boiled in fresh water until tender. The recipe makes enough for four to six people.

Lentil soup has long been popular in many different countries, and this traditional Spanish version is really rib-sticking and earthy. Serve with croûtons or buttered chunks of good homemade bread. This makes ample soup for four or six people.

☞ 3 tbsp. oil or butter
1 onion, peeled and chopped
2 carrots, scrubbed and chopped
1 garlic clove, peeled and chopped
14 oz. cooked red kidney beans
2 sprigs fresh thyme or generous pinch of dried thyme
½ tsp. cayenne
3 pints chicken stock
3 tsp. wine vinegar or cider vinegar
salt and freshly milled black pepper
some wild garlic leaves, thinly sliced or chopped
(or the green parts of some scallions or a small bunch of chives)

☞ 4 tbsp. olive oil
1 large onion, chopped
2 large carrots, peeled and chopped
1 celery stick, chopped
2 oz. raw Parma-style ham, cut into small scraps
a few parsley stalks
8 oz. green or brown lentils, washed
3 pints rich chicken stock
(preferably homemade)
salt and freshly milled black pepper

Heat the oil and sauté the onion, carrots and garlic for a few minutes or until soft and lightly colored. Add all but a generous handful of the kidney beans, stir, add the thyme and cayenne, and pour in the stock and vinegar. Bring to a boil, then reduce the heat, cover the pan and simmer for 45 minutes. Season generously. Allow to cool, then liquidize until smooth. Reheat gently, together with the reserved kidney beans. Just before serving, stir in the wild garlic, scallions or chives.

Heat the oil in a large, steep-sided pan and fry the onion for 2–3 minutes. Add the carrots, celery, ham and parsley; stir-fry for 5 minutes longer. Add the lentils, sauté for 1 minute and then add the hot stock. Bring to a boil, partially cover the pan and simmer for 50 minutes or until the lentils are soft. Season to taste and leave the soup to cool, then liquidize it in a food processor. Add a little extra stock to thin the soup, if necessary. Reheat without boiling, remove the parsley and serve very hot. Note that once made, lentil soup tends to thicken up, so add more liquid when reheating.

A slightly hot, tart and very full-flavored soup made with convenient canned red kidney beans and flavored with pungent green alliums.

Curry spices give this thick parsnip soup real zest, the turmeric lending a wonderful warm colour.

SPICED PARSNIP SOUP

This recipe makes a thick spicy soup with a very creamy consistency, making enough for six or eight servings. Accompany with good crusty bread or croûtons.

☞ *4 tbs olive oil or 40 g/ 1½ oz butter*
1 large onion, peeled and chopped
1 kg/ 2¼ lb parsnips, peeled and cubed
1 celery stick, chopped
2 leeks, chopped
225 g/ 8 oz floury potatoes, peeled and cubed
2 tsp good quality curry powder
½ tsp cayenne
1 tsp ground mace
½ tsp turmeric
salt and freshly milled black pepper
1.7 litres/ 3 pints chicken stock
handful of fresh parsley or chives, chopped

Heat the oil or butter in a large pan and sauté all the vegetables over a medium heat for about 10 minutes, stirring constantly. Add the spices, season and stir. Pour in the stock, bring to the boil, cover the pan, reduce the heat and simmer for about 1 hour. Allow to cool slightly, then transfer the contents of the pan to the bowl of a food processor. Liquidize, then return to the pan and gently reheat without boiling. Check the seasoning, sprinkle with herbs and serve very hot. You can substitute a small amount of curry paste for the powder if preferred or omit the curry altogether.

A RICH PEPPER-WATER

This mulligatawny is generously spiced,
and thickened with a paste of nuts, herbs and garlic.

CURRIED SOUP

MULLIGATAWNY SOUP

Despite a shared ancestry with the peppery sambars of south-east India — the name derives from the Tamil for 'pepper-water' — Anglo-Indian mulligatawny soup became a favourite Victorian dish. Isabella Beeton, Eliza Acton, Charles Francatelli and Alexis Soyer all give recipes, but here is my own delicious version, in which the soup is thickened and enriched at the last moment with a paste of nuts, mint and garlic.

☞ 2–3 sprigs fresh mint or generous pinch of dried mint
2 tbs pine nuts or blanched almonds
3 garlic cloves, peeled
$\frac{1}{2}$ tsp salt
2 large onions, peeled
1 oven-ready free-range or corn-fed chicken
1 carrot, scrubbed and coarsely chopped
2 celery sticks
4 sprigs parsley
1 bay leaf
4 tbs peanut or sunflower oil
2 garlic cloves, peeled and crushed with a little salt
2 heaped tsp good quality Indian curry paste
2 tsp very fresh garam masala or curry powder
$\frac{1}{2}$ tsp turmeric
$\frac{1}{4}$ tsp cayenne
salt and plenty of freshly milled black pepper
juice of $\frac{1}{2}$ lemon

With a mortar and pestle pound the mint, nuts, whole garlic cloves and salt to a paste. Cut 1 of the onions into quarters.

Remove the breasts from the chicken and quarter them. Skin the chicken carcass and put it into a large pan together with the carrot, celery, parsley, bay leaf and onion quarters. Add 1.4 litres/2$\frac{1}{2}$ pints water, cover and bring to the boil. Simmer for about 1 hour to obtain a well-flavoured stock. Strain the stock.

Heat the oil in another pan large enough to accommodate all the stock. Slice the remaining onion and fry until golden brown. Now add the chicken breast pieces and fry until golden. Add the garlic, curry paste, garam masala, turmeric and cayenne, and season. Stirring well, pour in the chicken stock and lemon juice, and bring to the boil. Cover and simmer for about 15 minutes, then strain into another pan. Chop the chicken pieces and return to the soup. Serve at once in soup bowls, with rice and mango chutney.

A SOUP FOR CHRISTMAS

A very rich soup made with a quintessentially English trio of ingredients: Stilton cheese, celery, and walnuts, with a dash of port added for flavour and colour.

CELERY, STILTON AND WALNUT SOUP

*My delicious soup is perfect for Christmas suppers, as this
is the season when walnuts and Stilton are enjoyed most; the recipe
also has the virtue of using up any surplus Stilton as well as
crunchy celery which is the perfect foil for that rich fatty cheese.
Serves four.*

 25 g/ 1 oz butter
3 celery sticks, finely diced
1 garlic clove, peeled and finely chopped
110 g/ 4 oz Stilton, cubed
6 shelled walnuts, crushed or very finely chopped
salt and freshly milled black pepper
225 ml/ 8 fl oz milk
560 ml/ 1 pint hot chicken or vegetable stock
3 tbs port

Heat the butter in a pan and when just foaming, add the celery. Soften the celery over a medium heat for a few minutes, then add the garlic, mix well, and simmer for a minute longer. Add the cheese, and when almost melted, add the walnuts, season, and mix well. Pour in the milk, stock and port. Mix well, bring just to the boil, reduce to a simmer, and cook for 15 minutes. Check the seasoning and serve hot, with crusty bread. For a splendid pasta sauce omit the stock and celery and use half the milk.

STILTON CHEESE

Stilton cheese, or British Parmesan, as it is sometimes called, is generally preferred to all other cheeses by those whose authority few will dispute. Those made in May or June are usually served at Christmas; or, to be in prime order, should be kept from 10 to 12 months, or even longer. An artificial ripeness in Stilton cheese is sometimes produced by inserting a small piece of decayed Cheshire into an aperture at the top. From 3 weeks to a month is sufficient time to ripen the cheese. An additional flavour may also be obtained by scooping out a piece from the top, and pouring therein port, sherry, Madeira, or old ale, and letting the cheese absorb these for 2 or 3 weeks. But that cheese is the finest which is ripened without any artificial aid, is the opinion of those who are judges in these matters. In serving a Stilton cheese, the

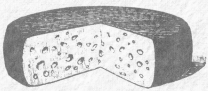

top of it should be cut off to form a lid, and a napkin or piece of white paper, with a frill at the top, pinned round. When the cheese goes from table, the lid should be replaced.

ISABELLA BEETON, *Book of Household Management (1861)*

A FRENCH FISHERMAN'S SOUP

MEDITERRANEAN FISH SOUP

*A very good soup so long as you use different
fish species, all in absolutely spanking fresh
condition. Pieces of filleted cod, hake, haddock,
monkfish, John Dory, grey mullet, etc. are all good.
Serve with rounds of fried bread and a garlicky
emulsion such as rouille or aïoli (see page 61).*

☞ *900 g/2 lb cleaned, filleted white-fleshed fish,
preferably mixed species*
salt
4 tbs olive oil
1 onion, peeled and chopped
4 garlic cloves, peeled and chopped
¼ tsp cayenne
white parts of 2 leeks, washed and sliced
1 carrot, scrubbed and chopped
1 red pepper, seeded, de-pithed and diced
400 g/14 oz canned plum tomatoes, chopped
2 bay leaves
sprigs of parsley, thyme and marjoram
large piece of lemon rind
560 ml/1 pint dry white wine
1.5 litres/3 pints water
½ tsp saffron threads
salt and freshly milled black pepper
1 tbs white wine vinegar

Salt the fish pieces. Heat the olive oil in a large pan. Add the onion, garlic, cayenne and the fresh vegetables; sauté until they just begin to colour, then add the fish, tomatoes, herbs, lemon rind, wine, water and saffron. Bring to the boil, cover, reduce the heat to medium and continue to cook fairly gently for 25 minutes.

Remove the herbs and the fish and any bones. If you like, keep the flesh to make the kedgeree or fish cake recipes but use up the next day.

Strain the soup into another pan, season well, add the vinegar and simmer for 10 minutes longer.

Meanwhile, make rouille or aïoli, and fry some bread rounds.

Ladle the soup into bowls and pass separately the bread, rouille or aïoli and a bowl of freshly grated cheese.

An opulent broth made with oysters, which were cheap and plentiful in Victorian times; mussels may be substituted.

OYSTER SOUP

ake eighty oysters and their liquor; place them in a pan with salt, cayenne pepper, and a teaspoon of chopped chervil; when boiling add three yolks of eggs beat up in half a pint of cream, and serve. This is enough for five persons. If the oysters have not sufficient liquor, a little water and salt may be added, and parsley may be used if preferred, instead of chervil.

LADY HARRIET ST CLAIR, *Dainty Dishes (1866)*

The classic Mediterranean sauces aïoli (large bowl) and fiery orange rouille (small bowl) both celebrate garlic, known to generations of well-bred English by its unkind epithet 'the stinking rose'.

AÏOLI

For all egg and oil emulsions it is essential that the eggs should be at or slightly above room temperature; cold or refrigerated eggs just won't work. Should the emulsion fail anyway, add a fresh egg yolk and whizz again until thick.

☞ *3 garlic cloves, peeled*
1 tsp salt
2 egg yolks
2 tbs wine vinegar
200 ml/7 fl oz olive oil

Crush the garlic to a paste with the salt. Put the crushed garlic, egg yolks, vinegar and 1 tbs of the oil into a food processor. With the motor running, add the remaining oil in a very thin stream; stop when the mixture is thick and glossy. Serve in a bowl.

ROUILLE

More fiery than aïoli, rouille is a French accompaniment to fish soups.

☞ *140 ml/5 fl oz olive oil*
2 garlic cloves, peeled
½ tsp cayenne
1 tsp paprika
2 egg yolks
salt to taste

Heat 2 tsp of the oil in a small pan and very gently simmer the garlic, cayenne and paprika over a low heat for 30 seconds, stirring constantly. Combine in the bowl of a food processor everything except half of the remaining oil. With the motor running, add the rest of the oil in a very thin stream. Stop as soon as the rouille is thick and shiny. Serve in a bowl.

GARLIC – The smell of this plant is generally considered offensive, and it is the most acrimonious in its taste of the whole of the alliaceous tribe. In 1548 it was introduced to England from the shores of the Mediterranean, where it is abundant, and in Sicily it grows naturally. It was in greater repute with our ancestors than it is with ourselves, although it is still used as a seasoning herb. On the continent, especially in Italy, it is much used, and the French consider it an essential in many made dishes.

ISABELLA BEETON, *Book of Household Management (1861)*

STOCKS

VEGETABLE STOCK

☞ 4 tbs olive oil

2 onions, peeled and quartered

2–3 leeks, chopped

4 carrots, chopped

5–6 celery sticks, chopped

8 parsley stalks with their leaves

1 tbs tomato pureé

salt and freshly milled black pepper

2 litres/3½ pints water

Put everything into a large pan and bring to the boil. Cover, reduce the heat and simmer for 1 hour. Check the seasoning, strain and refrigerate for 24 hours (or freeze until required).

CHICKEN STOCK

This well-flavoured stock is worth making whenever you have a fresh chicken carcass; a cooked one will give far less flavour. I use this as the basis of many soups, stews and risotti. Substitute other fowl for a game stock.

☞ 1 chicken carcass, preferably uncooked

2 large onions, peeled and quartered

2 large carrots, peeled and chopped

2 celery sticks, chopped

small bunch of fresh parsley (stalks and leaves)

12 black peppercorns

2 bay leaves

salt

2 litres/3½ pints water

Put all the ingredients into a very large pan and bring to the boil. Cover, reduce the heat and simmer, skimming off the scum as it rises. After about 2 hours the stock will be ready. Allow it to cool, pour off any fat and strain. Refrigerate for 24 hours or pour into freezer bags, seal and freeze until required.

Cook's Tip

Too many starchy root vegetables will make stock cloudy, even though the taste will not be adversely affected.

Real home-made vegetable and chicken stocks are indispensable in all manner of Victorian dishes, and they are always preferable to stock cubes for optimum flavour.

Part Four
SALADS, VEGETABLES & ACCOMPANIMENTS

THIS CHAPTER is something of a miscellany, but a fine, rich one at that. It brings together a diverse collection of salads, vegetable dishes and rice accompaniments. All are excellent served either with main courses or as first courses. Some, such as the calf's liver salad and the traditional French dandelion salad, are really a meal in themselves, and are perfectly attuned to the current preference for lighter, healthy eating.

Individual vegetables shine in this chapter, and in sourcing the recipes I have allowed my particular passions to choose for me. So I make no apologies for the abundant potato recipes such as a sharp potato salad, and the light, moist potato rissoles; nor for the mushrooms, stewed and grilled. Asparagus is so delicious that, when in season, I gorge on it every day, whether in a simple sauce of melted butter or baked in the Italian manner. My favourite is classic Boston baked beans recipe.

Last but not least come the tender, creamy, exquisite Milanese risotto, followed by three different pilaff recipes, the ideal accompaniments to any of the Indian-influenced or spicier main course dishes to be found in Parts Six, Seven and Eight of this book.

A TANGY, COLD WEATHER ACCOMPANIMENT

In Eliza Acton's 'Dressed Cucumbers' ribbons of cool raw cucumbers contrast with cayenne pepper in a sharp dressing. This salad is an excellent enlivener.

INDIAN SALADO

Slice two cucumbers without seeds, a Spanish onion, two rennets, and two chillies. Season with pepper and salt, and stir together, and add two spoonfuls of vinegar, and three of salad oil. The cut meat of a lobster, or of crabs' claws, may be put to this, and cayenne. The onion may be omitted at pleasure.

MEG DODS, *Cook and Housewife's Manual (1829)*

DRESSED CUCUMBERS

Cut into lengths of an inch or rather more, one or two freshly grated Cucumbers, take off the rind, and then pare them round and round into thin ribbons, until the watery part is reached; this is to be thrown aside. When all done, sprinkle them with cayenne and fine salt, and leave them to drain a little; then arrange them lightly in a clean dish, and sauce them with very fine oil, well mixed with chilli vinegar, or with equal parts of chilli and of common vinegar.

Cucumbers, 2 or 3; salt, 1 to 2 saltspoonsful; little cayenne; oil, 6 to 8 tablespoonsful; chilli vinegar, or equal parts of this and common vinegar, 2 to 4 tablespoonsful.

ELIZA ACTON,
Modern Cookery for Private Families (1855)

Cook's Tip

Eliza Acton's own 'receipt' from Modern Cookery makes an excellent salad or vegetable accompaniment to cold beef, ham or chicken, although the amount of dressing may be considered a little excessive. Assuming that you have 2 large cucumbers, I prefer just 4 tbs of olive oil beaten with 1 or 2 of good wine vinegar. Judging by the cayenne and chilli vinegar, she evidently liked it hot! Those with more delicate palates may sprinkle a very light dusting of cayenne over the cucumbers and use plain vinegar. The addition of a very finely sliced spring onion and a little chopped fresh mint further enhances the dish.

SUMMER SALAD

Rinse and well shake off all moisture from a couple of Cos lettuce, cut them up into a bowl or basin, add a few roughly-chopped green onions, half a gill of cream, a table-spoonful of vinegar, pepper and salt to taste. Mix all together.

BACON SALAD

Having prepared any kind of salad you may happen to have, such as endive, corn salad, lettuce, celery, mustard and cress, seasoned with beet-root, onions, or shalot; let the salad be cut up into a bowl or basin ready for seasoning in the following manner: cut eight ounces of fat bacon into small square pieces the size of a cob-nut, fry these in a frying-pan, and as soon as they are done, pour the whole upon the salad; add two table-spoonfuls of vinegar, pepper and salt to taste. Mix thoroughly.

PLAIN SALAD

Cos lettuce cut up in a bowl or basin, seasoned with chopped green mint and green onions, a spoonful of moist sugar, vinegar, pepper and salt. Mix thoroughly.

CELERY CRAB SALAD

First thoroughly wash and wipe clean, and then cut a stick of celery into a basin; add two ounces of any kind of cheese sliced very thinly, season with a good teaspoonful of made mustard, a table-spoonful of salad oil, ditto of vinegar, with pepper and salt. Mix thoroughly.

The 'plain' salad could do with 2–3 tbs of oil added to the dressing, and I can find no explanation for the curious name of the last salad.

A crisp salad of Cos lettuce with a sharp cream dressing; the bowl below shows the curiously named 'celery crab salad', in which crab meat is entirely absent. All the recipes are from Francatelli's A Plain Cookery Book for the Working Classes.

An elegant calf's liver salad. Although this has become a signature dish of many contemporary chefs, this recipe has the hallmarks of the best of Victorian English cookery.

CALF'S LIVER SALAD

This substantial salad makes an excellent appetizer or light lunch for two people. The idea of cooking the liver with fines herbes was inspired by Mrs Beeton.

☞ *225 g/8 oz well-trimmed calf's liver*
freshly milled black pepper
flour, for dusting the liver
2 sprigs tarragon
3 sprigs parsley
3 sprigs chervil
small bunch of chives
some exotic salad leaves such as oak leaf lettuce, radicchio, frisée lettuce
few sprigs of watercress, stems trimmed
1–2 tbs extra virgin olive oil, walnut or hazelnut oil
50 g/2 oz butter or 4–5 tbs olive oil
2 shallots, peeled and very finely chopped
1 tbs red wine vinegar or sherry vinegar
salt

Wash the calf's liver, which should be completely free of tubes. Slice into strips. Dip them in freshly milled pepper and flour. Wash the herbs, salad leaves and the watercress. Shake dry; chop the herbs finely and tear the salad leaves roughly. Dress the salad leaves with extra virgin olive oil or nut oil and combine in a salad bowl or on two plates.

Heat most of the butter or olive oil in a frying pan. Put in the sliced calf's liver and fry gently for just 1 or 2 minutes on each side, depending upon the size of the strips. Remove and scatter over the dressed salad. Add a little extra butter or oil to the pan, then the shallots, chopped herbs and vinegar. Season with a little salt and reduce. Pour the contents of the pan over the salad and eat at once.

Cook's Tip
Calf's liver must be only briefly fried or it will become tough.

A LIGHT LUNCH

SALADE DE PISSENLITS

This traditional rustic salad makes an excellent light lunch or vegetable accompaniment. The French name for dandelion alludes honestly to its powerful diuretic properties. Conversely, the English word comes from the French dent de lion, or lion's tooth, which accurately describes the lovely serrated shape of the leaves. Pick the wild plants before they flower, otherwise they will be too bitter. Spring and autumn are the best times to gather young dandelions. This is enough for two people.

☞ *350 g/ 12 oz freshly picked young dandelion plants*
3 tbs olive oil
175 g/ 6 oz streaky bacon, cut into small strips
3 tbs red or white wine vinegar
salt and freshly milled black pepper
small bunch of chives, chopped

Trim away the bottom part of the dandelion roots, wash the plants very thoroughly, then shake them dry. Put them in a salad bowl. Heat the oil in a small non-stick frying pan. Fry the bacon until crisp, then empty the pan contents into the salad bowl.

Add the vinegar to the pan, reheat and stir for a few seconds while it bubbles, then pour over the salad. Season, sprinkle with chives and eat straight away.

NOTE: other bitter green salad leaves may be substituted for the dandelions.

Cook's Tip

For a more substantial salad, add any or all of the following: a chopped hard-boiled egg, a sliced spring onion, a sliced cooked beetroot or some cubes of fried bread.

The mildly bitter leaves of wild dandelions dressed with crisp morsels of fried bacon and dressed with a sharp vinaigrette make a delicious salad for spring and early autumn.

A LIGHT AND TANGY POTATO SALAD

Whole, unpeeled new potatoes are lightly boiled, tossed while still warm in a mustard vinaigrette, then finished with a dressing of sour cream and fresh herbs.

POTATO SALAD

My relatively light but tangy potato salad is best made with very small new potatoes, of which there are many good varieties; 'Pink fir apple' is an excellent, well-flavoured main crop variety that works perhaps best of all. This salad serves four people.

☞ 675 g/ 1½ lb baby new potatoes, well washed but left unpeeled
3 tbs olive oil
2 tbs white wine vinegar
1 tsp prepared English mustard
salt and freshly milled black pepper
140 ml/ 4 fl oz sour cream
small bunch of fresh chives, snipped
leaves from 3 sprigs of mint, chopped

Boil the potatoes until tender but do not over-cook them. Drain well, then put them in a bowl. Beat the olive oil with the vinegar, mustard and seasoning. Pour it over the potatoes while they are still hot, turning them to coat. When they have cooled, fold in the sour cream. Add the chives and mint, season lightly, and mix thoroughly. Serve immediately or refrigerate until the salad is required.

RECIPE FOR A SALAD

To make this condiment your poet begs
The pounded yellow of two hard-boil'd eggs;
Two boiled potatoes, passed through kitchen sieve,
Smoothness and softness to the salad give.
Let onion atoms lurk within the bowl,
And, half-suspected, animate the whole.
Of mordant mustard add a single spoon,
Distrust the condiment that bites so soon;
But deem it not, thou man of herbs, a fault
To add a double quantity of salt;
Four times the spoon with oil of Lucca crown,
And twice with vinegar, procur'd from town;
And lastly o'er the flavour'd compound toss
a magic soupçon of anchovy sauce.
Oh, green and glorious! Oh, herbaceous treat!
Twould tempt the dying anchorite to eat;
Back to the world he'd turn his fleeting soul,
And plunge his fingers in the salad-bowl!
Serenely full, the epicure would say
'Fate cannot harm me, I have dined to-day.'

SYDNEY SMITH, *Selected Letters*

POTATO RISSOLES

Adapted from Eliza Acton's Modern Cookery for Private Families, *these tasty rissoles are quite similar to traditional French potato croquettes. They are very good with any poultry or meat dish, accompanied by a green vegetable such as spinach, broccoli or courgettes. Alternatively enjoy them as a snack. This makes 6-8 rissoles.*

☞ *450 g / 1 lb floury potatoes, peeled*
25 g / 1 oz butter or 1 tbs olive oil
2 tbs milk
salt and freshly milled black pepper
25 g / 1 oz Parma ham, very finely chopped
handful of fresh parsley, finely chopped
2 spring onions or 1 shallot, peeled and very finely chopped
flour for coating
olive oil for frying

Boil the potatoes until tender. Mash them with the butter or olive oil and milk. Allow to cool slightly, then season with salt and pepper and mix in the ham, parsley and spring onions or shallot. Shape the mixture into balls – slightly larger than golf balls – and roll them in flour. Heat a layer of olive oil in a non-stick frying pan. Fry the rissoles in batches over a medium heat, turning so that they become evenly golden. Drain on kitchen paper and eat them very hot.

Cook's Tip

For an excellent Indian version, just omit the ham and substitute a pinch of cayenne, 1 tsp curry powder (or garam masala), and replace the parsley with fresh coriander. Otherwise, proceed as directed in the recipe for Potato Rissoles.

Light and fluffy rissoles and croquettes have always been popular in many European cuisines, and they are an economical way to use up leftover mashed potatoes.

Nutty new potatoes are delicious enough served piping hot, with just a pat of butter to melt over them and a good dusting of freshly ground black pepper. When dressed and heated through with well-seasoned, spiced cream and lemon juice, they are elevated to a delectable feast.

NEW POTATOES À LA CRÈME

❧

Cut some recently-boiled new potatoes in slices, put them into a stewpan with a gill of cream, 4 oz. of fresh butter, a very little nutmeg, pepper and salt, and the juice of half a lemon; set them to boil on the stove-fire, toss them well together, and dish them up with croûtons.

CHARLES ELMÉ FRANCATELLI, *The Modern Cook (1896 edition)*

OF THE STREET TRADE IN BAKED POTATOES

The customers consist of all classes. Many gentlefolks buy them in the streets, and take them home for supper in their pockets; but the working classes are the greatest purchasers. Many boys and girls lay out a halfpenny in a baked potato. Irishmen are particularly fond of them, but they are the worst customers, I am told, as they want the largest potatoes in the can. Women buy a great number of those sold. Some take them home, and some eat them in the street. Three baked potatoes are as much as will satisfy the stoutest appetite.

HENRY MAYHEW, *London Labour And The London Poor*

POTATOES À LA MAÎTRE D'HÔTEL

❧

INGREDIENTS – *Potatoes, salt and water; to every 6 potatoes allow 1 tablespoonful of minced parsley, 2 oz. of butter, pepper and salt to taste, 4 tablespoonfuls of gravy, 2 tablespoonfuls of lemon-juice.*

MODE – Wash the potatoes clean, and boil them in salt and water...when they are done, drain them, let them cool; then peel and cut the potatoes into thick slices: if these are too thin, they would break in the sauce. Put the butter into a stewpan with the pepper, salt, gravy, and parsley; mix these ingredients well together, put in the potatoes, shake them two or three times, that they may be well covered with the sauce, and, when quite hot through, squeeze in the lemon-juice, and serve.

ISABELLA BEETON, *Book of Household Management (1861)*

COOKING WITH 'THE GOLDEN APPLE'

The following tomato dishes are original Shaker recipes that were published in the journal The Manifesto *in 1880, and also appear in* The Best of Shaker Cooking *by Amy Bess Miller and Percy Fuller (Macmillan, 1985). Each one demonstrates the care and attention that Shaker sisters lavished upon fresh home-grown ingredients, and the recipes could almost be contemporary. The Shakers were among the first to market their canned and preserved fruit and vegetables, which were famous for their excellent flavour.*

STEWED TOMATOES

Stew tomatoes in water to cover in a porcelain stewpan, having first removed the skins and pits of the tomatoes. Allow to boil briskly partially covered for 20 minutes. Then remove to back of stove to simmer slowly until required. Season liberally with butter, salt, and pepper. They will be cooked to a creamy consistency and will not need flour or cracker crumbs, which to our taste are no improvement. Cook slowly at least 2 hours. Watch heat as tomatoes burn suddenly.

BROILED TOMATOES

Cut small tomatoes in halves and place upon a wire gridiron cut surface down; when the surface is somewhat cooked, turn tomatoes with the skin towards the fire and finish cooking, about 5 more minutes; serve hot with butter, salt and pepper upon each half. These make a nice garnish for broiled steak.

Large tomato varieties such as the ubiquitous beefsteak are better stuffed and lightly baked or braised than eaten raw, as in this delicious American recipe.

MUSHROOMS

A traditional Italian dish of firm wild fungi such as ceps or meadow mushrooms, grilled with a stuffing of garlic, shallots, parsley and breacrumbs, and liberally doused in fruity olive oil; large cultivated mushrooms are almost as delicious cooked in this way.

THE PEARL OF THE FIELDS

I here send you, Eloise, a most sumptuous dish. There is one dish in which the Devonshire cottager can procure and enjoy better than even the most wealthy person. It is the mushroom. After having plucked them, perhaps on the road home for his breakfast, broiled them over a nice bright fire, seasoned with a little pepper and salt, and a small bit of butter placed inside of them; the flavour is then pure and the aroma beautiful...

ALEXIS SOYER, *A Shilling Cookery for the People (1859)*

Choose large, firm, fresh-gathered flaps. Skin them, and score the under side. Put them into an earthen dish, and baste them with oil or melted butter, and strew pepper and salt over them. When they have been steeped in this marinade for an hour or more, broil them on both sides over a clear fire, and serve them with a sauce of oil or melted butter, minced parsley, young onions, a little garlic, and the juice of a lemon, poured over them; or they may be done in the oven, and a sauce drawn from their trimmings and stalks.

MEG DODS, *Cook and Housewife's Manual (1829)*

GRILLED MUSHROOMS

Choose large, firm flat cap mushrooms for this; wild agaricus campestris or agaricus arvensis are most delicious of all but cultivated ones are also very good. Serve one large or two smaller caps per person, and crusty bread to mop up the juices.

4–8 large mushrooms, wiped clean
2–4 garlic cloves, peeled and finely chopped
2 shallots, peeled and very finely chopped
4 generous handfuls fresh parsley
2–4 tbs very fine fresh breadcrumbs
extra virgin olive oil
salt and freshly milled black pepper

Preheat the grill. Remove the stems from the mushrooms and, if loose, peel off the skins. Mix together the garlic, shallots, parsley and breadcrumbs. Place the mushrooms in a clean, shallow container, the gills facing up. Drizzle a little olive oil over them and season with salt and pepper. Grill for about 3 minutes, then invert the mushrooms, pour a little more oil over the caps, and season. Grill for 4 minutes, then invert the mushrooms again so that the partly-cooked gill sides face up. Spoon the parsley mixture into the cavities and sprinkle a little more oil over them; grill again for 2–3 minutes longer, then serve immediately.

MUSHROOMS FROM THE FIELDS

Here, fresh closed cap mushrooms have been stewed gently in butter, lemon juice and milk, and seasoned with salt, pepper and grated nutmeg.

VARIETIES OF THE MUSHROOM – The common mushroom found in our pastures is the Agaricus campestris of science, and another edible British species is A. Georgii; but A. primulus is affirmed to be the most delicious mushroom. The morel is Morchella esculenta, and Tuber cibarium is the common truffle. There is in New Zealand a long fungus, which grows from the head of a caterpillar, and which forms a horn, as it were, and is called Sphaeria Robertsii.

ISABELLA BEETON, *Book of Household Management (1861)*

84

STEWED MUSHROOMS

INGREDIENTS – *1 pint mushroom-buttons, 3 oz. fresh butter, white pepper and salt to taste, lemon-juice, 1 tablespoon of flour, cream or milk, ¼ teaspoonful of grated nutmeg.*

MODE – Cut off the ends of the stalks, and pare neatly a pint of mushroom buttons; put them into a basin of water, with a little lemon-juice, as they are done. When all are prepared, take them from the water with the hands, to avoid the sediment, and put them into a stewpan with the fresh butter, white pepper, salt, and the juice of ½ lemon; cover the pan closely, and let the mushrooms stew gently from 20–25 minutes; then thicken the butter with the above proportion of flour, add gradually sufficient cream, or cream and milk, to make the sauce of a proper consistency, and put in the grated nutmeg. If the mushrooms are not perfectly tender, stew them for 5 minutes longer, remove every particle of butter which may be floating on top, and serve.

ISABELLA BEETON, *Book of Household Management (1861)*

Cook's Tip

I would never soak mushrooms in water, which makes them soggy, preferring instead to wipe them clean with a damp cloth. For contemporary tastes the quantity of butter seems a little extravagant, and in any case the health-conscious may prefer to substitute olive oil or a mixture of oil and butter; I suggest 2–3 tbs oil for 225 g/ 8 oz medium-size closed cup mushrooms, cut in half. (Increase the mushrooms if they are tiny buttons but leave them whole.) This is roughly equivalent to 1 pint. Nor do I like to thicken the mushrooms with flour, which I find cloying. In fact I have cooked this dish perfectly without flour and with just 4 tbs cream and some fresh chopped parsley stirred in for the last two minutes of cooking. A very good variation can be made with a little chicken stock – about half a teacup – in place of the cream, but this should be added early on together with the lemon juice.

ASPARAGUS - SPRING'S GLORY

Although delicious served cold with vinaigrette, hollandaise or mayonnaise, nothing beats the warm shoots simply dressed with plenty of melted butter and a good sprinkling of black pepper.

The greatest defect of the English arrangement of dinner is that almost always vegetables are of no account except as adjuncts. It is not understood, except in the dinners of the poor, that a vegetable may make an excellent dish to be eaten by itself alone. To this rule, however, there are two exceptions made – in favour of artichokes and asparagus. It is a question whether this exception is due to a pure admiration of the vegetable, or due to the circumstances that, having to be eaten with the fingers, it is necessary to put down either knife or fork in order to seize the vegetable. The probability is, that if the Creator had thought fit, in His wisdom, to endow the Englishman with three or four hands, he would never be seen eating the artichoke or the asparagus alone, but always in conjunction with some other food.

E. S. DALLAS, *Kettner's Book of the Table (1877)*

GRATIN OF ASPARAGUS

This is inspired by traditional Italian recipes, and is best served as an appetiser or as a vegetable to accompany a meaty main course. Serves two people.

☞ *1 bundle asparagus (about 225 g/8 oz)*
salt and freshly milled black pepper
15 g/½ oz butter
15 g/½ oz Parmesan cheese, freshly grated

Preheat the oven to 200°C/400°F/gas mark 6. Trim off the woody, bottom parts of the stems, then parboil the asparagus in plenty of boiling salted water, and drain well. Butter a shallow ovenproof dish. Lay in the asparagus, season with salt and pepper, and dot with the butter. Sprinkle with cheese and bake until the cheese has melted and turned pale golden.

ASPARAGUS – This plant belongs to the variously-featured family of the order Liliaceae, which, in the temperate regions of both hemispheres, are most abundant, and, between the tropics, gigantic in size and arborescent in form. Asparagus is native of Great Britain, and is found on various parts of the seacoast, and in the fens of Lincolnshire. At Kynarve Cove in Cornwall, there is an island called 'Asparagus Island', from the abundance in which it is there found. The uses to which the young shoots are applied, and the manure in which they are cultivated in order to bring them to the highest state of excellence, have been a study with many kitchen-gardeners.

ISABELLA BEETON,
Book of Household Management (1861)

ASPARAGUS WITH MELTED BUTTER

Asparagus was just as prized in Victorian times as it is today. Then, it was popular boiled and dished up on toasted bread, with melted butter; both Eliza Acton and Alexis Soyer give recipes, and they remark upon the French preference for cold asparagus dressed with vinaigrette; cold cooked asparagus is also excellent with hollandaise or mayonnaise. Asparagus soup coloured with spinach was also popular. This recipe is for two people.

☞ *1 bundle asparagus (about 225 g/8 oz)*
40 g/1½ oz butter
salt and freshly milled black pepper

Trim off the woody base of the stems but keep the asparagus tied up in a bundle. Bring plenty of salted water to a rolling boil, put in the asparagus and cook until tender; this usually takes 6–12 minutes, depending upon their thickness. Meanwhile gently melt the butter. Drain the asparagus and arrange in a fan on a plate. Pour over the melted butter and season with salt and pepper.

Cook's Tip
A little chopped Parma ham or diced fried bacon are excellent additions.

I revere the memory of Mr F as an estimable man and most indulgent husband, only necessary to mention Asparagus and it appeared...

CHARLES DICKENS, *Little Dorrit (1857)*

THE PILGRIM FATHERS' BEAN FEAST

HOMEMADE BAKED BEANS

☞ *175 g/ 6 oz dried haricot (navy) beans*
175 g/ 6 oz streaky bacon
1 small onion, peeled
1 tbs maple syrup or black treacle
2–3 tsp mustard powder
2 cloves
1 tsp salt
1 tbs tomato purée (optional)
freshly milled black pepper

Soak the beans overnight in cold water. Drain them. Preheat the oven to 150°C/300°F/gas mark 2. Put the beans into a large casserole or earthenware pot and add all the other ingredients, mixing thoroughly. Boil enough water to cover and pour over the beans.

Mix well, burying the onion. Bake for 6 hours or until the beans are very soft, topping up with boiling water whenever necessary. Check the seasoning, discard the onion, and serve hot with thick buttered chunks of wholemeal bread.

BOSTON BAKED BEANS

Pick over one quart pea beans, cover with cold water, and soak over night. In morning, drain, cover with fresh water, heat slowly (keeping water below boiling point), and cook until skins will burst - which is best determined by taking a few beans on the tip of a spoon and blowing on them, when skins will burst if sufficiently cooked. Beans thus tested must, of course, be thrown away. Drain beans, throwing bean water out of doors, not in sink. Scald rind of one-half pound fat salt pork, scrape, remove one-fourth inch slice and put in bottom of bean-pot. Cut through rind of remaining pork every one-half-inch, making cuts one inch deep. Put beans in pot and bury pork in beans, leaving rind exposed. Mix one tablespoon salt, one tablespoon molasses, and three tablespoons sugar; add one cup boiling water, and pour over beans; then add more boiling water to cover beans. Cover bean-pot, put in oven, and bake slowly six or eight hours, uncovering the last hour of cooking, that rind may become browned and crisp. Add water as needed. Many feel sure that by adding with seasonings one-half tablespoon mustard, the beans are more easily digested.

FANNIE FARMER, *The Boston Cooking School Cook Book (1896)*

Baked beans have been linked to Boston ever since the first Puritans landed there, bringing dried beans with them from England. Ironically all but one bean species (vicia fava, the broad or fava bean) are native to the Americas. Strict observers of the Sabbath, the Boston Puritans baked beans on Saturdays and so were able to eat on Sundays without the need to cook since cooking, which was considered work, was banned. Baked beans remained popular in American households throughout the Victorian era, and were eventually canned commercially by Messrs Heinz. This serves two people.

THE MILANESE ARISTOCRAT

*This is perhaps the supreme rice dish, a wonderfully creamy and
well-flavoured risotto that celebrates just a handful of really fine ingredients.*

RISOTTO ALLA MILANESE

I am always struck by the simplicity, freshness and enduring relevance of Eliza Acton's marvellous 'receipts'. In 1855, ten years after the first publication of her book **Modern Cookery**, *she added a chapter on 'foreign and Jewish cookery'. This serves four people.*

☞ *½ tsp saffron strands*
1.1 litres/2 pints chicken stock), kept hot
75 g/3 oz butter
1 large onion, peeled and finely chopped
300 g/11 oz arborio rice
50 g/2 oz Parmesan cheese, freshly grated

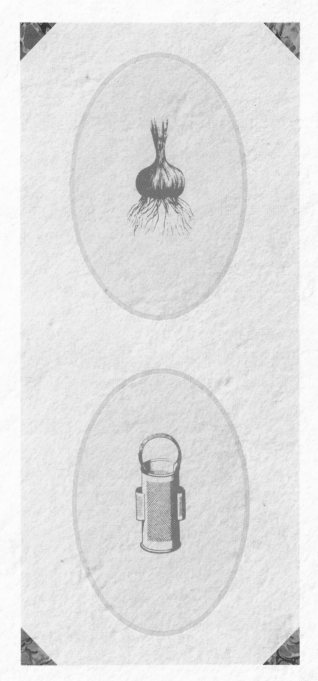

Steep the saffron in the hot stock for at least 10 minutes. Meanwhile, heat half of the butter in a wide, heavy-bottomed pan. As soon as it froths, add the onion. Sauté until golden, then add the rice and turn it in the fat for about 2 minutes. Add some of the stock, mix well and raise the heat. Stirring frequently, cook uncovered until the stock has been absorbed, then add a little more. Repeat, stirring often to loosen any rice at the bottom of the pan, until all the stock has been used up and the rice is tender: about 25 minutes. Season, stir in the remaining butter, all the Parmesan, and serve 'very hot, at the commencement of dinner as a potage'.

OBS – The reader should bear in mind what we have so often repeated in this volume, that rice should always be perfectly cooked, and that it will not become tender with less than three times its bulk in liquid.

ELIZA ACTON, *Modern Cookery for Private Families (1855)*

Cook's Tip
Home-made stock is best for this relatively simple but delicious dish. Each time stock is added let the rice absorb virtually all the liquid before adding more.

RICE AND SPICE

PILAU RICE

Indian pilaus are dishes of long-grain rice fried with onion and whole spices and simmered in water or stock. Nuts are often included, raisins or sultanas may be added, as may aromatic leaves such as bay or curry leaf, and pilaus are sometimes coloured yellow with turmeric. They are obviously closely related to the delicate, aromatic pilaffs of the Middle East, Turkey and central Asia, which sometimes include morsels of meat or poultry. This standard recipe serves four, and is the ideal accompaniment to all the Indian dishes in the book.

☞ *350 g/12 oz basmati rice*
15 g/½ oz butter or ghee or 2 tbs vegetable oil
1 small onion, peeled and chopped
2 oz flaked blanched almonds
1 cinnamon stick
4 cloves
6 whole green cardamom pods
1 large dried red chilli
1 tsp salt
560 ml/1 pint chicken stock or water

Wash the rice in several changes of fresh cold water, gently squeezing the grains to release some starch. When the water is no longer cloudy, drain the rice well.

Heat the butter, ghee or oil in a saucepan with a tight-fitting lid. Fry the onion, almonds, spices and whole chilli until the onion is golden, then add the rice and stir around for a minute or two. Add the salt and stock or water, bring to the boil, then cover the pan, reduce the heat to minimum and cook for 20 minutes. The rice should be dry and tender.

RICE

This is a plant of Indian origin, and has formed the principal food of the Indian and Chinese people from the most remote antiquity. Both Pliny and Dioscorides class it with the cereals, though Galen places it among the vegetables. Be this as it may, however, it was imported to Greece, from India, about 286 years before Christ, and by the ancients it was esteemed both nutritious and fattening.

ISABELLA BEETON, *Book of Household Management (1861)*

The classic Indian pilau; spiced with fragrant cinnamon, whole cloves, cardamom and dried chilli peppers, and textured with crunchy nuts is a fine partner for all manner of Indian curries, highly spiced stews, and simple grilled kebabs.

ELEGANT PILAFF

The warm glow and subtle flavour of saffron make this pilaff an elegant accompaniment to simple grilled meat or poultry dishes.

A PILAU – Stew some rice in broth, or with butter; and season it with white pepper, mace, cayenne, and cloves. Place two small fowls, or a few veal or mutton cutlets, in the centre of a large dish, and lay some slices of boiled bacon beside them. Cover with rice; smooth and glaze the rice with egg, and set the dish before the fire or in the oven, to brown for a while. Garnish with yolks of hard-boiled eggs and fried onions, or use forcemeat-balls.

OBS – This is no bad dish, whatever country owns it. A more oriental complexion may be given to this dish by frying the rice in butter, stirring it with a fork till of a light-brown, and then stewing it in broth till soft.

MEG DODS, *Cook and Housewife's Manual (1829)*

SAFFRON PILAFF

This is more delicate and elegant than the Indian pilau. Serve it with any poultry dish; it perfectly complements barbecued chicken or spicy lamb kebabs. This serves four.

350 g/12 oz long-grain rice
560 ml/1 pint chicken stock
½–¾ tsp saffron threads
salt and freshly milled black pepper
50 g/2 oz pine nuts, toasted
2 spring onions, very thinly sliced
small handful of fresh parsley, chopped

Soak the rice in several changes of fresh water, squeezing gently with your hand to release the starch. Rinse several times and drain well.

Bring the stock to a simmer in a covered pan. Add the saffron, season, turn off the heat and leave to infuse for 10 minutes. Add the drained rice and bring to the boil. Cover tightly, reduce the heat to minimum and cook for 15 minutes.

Mix in the pine nuts, spring onions and parsley.

FROM MR. LANE, THE ORIENTAL TRAVELLER

Pilaw or pilau is made by boiling rice in plenty of water for about twenty minutes, so that the water drains off easily, leaving the grains whole, and with some degree of hardness; then stirring it up with a little butter, just enough to make the grains separate easily and seasoning it with salt and pepper. Often a fowl, boiled almost to rags, is laid on top. Sometimes small morsels of fried or roasted mutton or lamb are mixed with it; and there are many other additions; but generally the Turks and Arabs add nothing to the rice but the butter, and salt, and pepper.

ELIZA ACTON,
Modern Cookery for Private Families (1855)

Part Five
EGGS & PASTA

EGGS CAN be baked, either simply, with butter, cream and grated cheese, or more elaborately, as in the Spanish recipe for eggs warmly flavoured with air-dried ham, onion, tomatoes, peppers and paprika. Avoiding the over-familiar and the obvious, I have chosen eggs in brown butter and capers to represent frying; to scrambled eggs I have added a delicious topping of sautéed mushrooms flavoured with truffle oil. Soufflés were popular with the Victorians, and I give three recipes: one plain, another delicately flavoured and coloured with spinach, a third masquerading as a 'fondu'. Omelettes were also favoured, even if spelled differently and also sometimes called by the alternative name of 'fraise'. Altogether, Victorians were experts at egg cuisine.

Although the choice of excellent pasta varieties is now almost bewildering, Victorian cooks in Britain were familiar with but a handful, of which macaroni was the most popular and commonly available. These limitations notwithstanding, their recipes are very good, even when judged by today's flamboyant, cosmopolitan standards. I particularly recommend my versions of rich 'dressed' macaroni, and pasta in a bacon, cream and asparagus sauce, supposedly invented in the nineteenth century by one Aurelio Saffi.

Sharpened with capers and vinegar, this excellent dish of eggs in brown butter was much loved by Victorian cooks.

EXCELLENT EGGS TO SAVOUR

EGGS WITH BROWN BUTTER

This very simple savoury egg dish serves two people, accompanied by crusty bread.

———————

☞ *2 tsp capers*
25 g/ 1oz butter
4 free-range eggs
small handful of fresh parsley, chopped
salt and freshly milled black pepper
1 tbs white wine vinegar

———————

If salted, thoroughly rinse and drain the capers. Chop them. Heat half the butter in a non-stick frying pan. When foaming add the eggs and the parsley, season and fry for about two minutes. With a spoon baste the eggs with hot butter. When done, carefully lift the eggs on to a warmed serving dish, then add the rest of the butter to the pan together with the capers. When the butter is light brown (not burnt) add the vinegar, season again and stir. Pour the brown butter over the eggs and eat straight away.

ASPARAGUS AND EGGS

Asparagus and Eggs – Beat three or four eggs well with pepper and salt. Cut some dressed asparagus into pieces the size of pease, and stir them into the eggs. Melt two ounces of butter in a small stew-pan, and pouring in the mixture, stir it till it thickens, and serve it hot on a toast.

MEG DODS, *Cook and Housewife's Manual (1829)*

Cook's Tip

This makes a kind of asparagus omelette. For a five-egg omelette, parboil 110 g/4 oz trimmed asparagus until tender, drain, then dice it small and stir into the beaten egg. Let the butter get very hot in a large non-stick frying pan but do not let it burn; a mixture of olive oil and butter may be preferred. Cook the eggs like a normal omelette, folded in half, but with a moist interior. Divide into two servings and eat as soon as cooked, with crusty bread. Variation: beat the eggs with 1 tbs milk or cream, then scramble with a little butter, season well, and divide into two portions. Serve on hot buttered toast, and top with the cooked, diced asparagus.

SPANISH BAKED EGGS

The original version of this popular and very traditional Spanish dish was probably introduced by the Moors since, without the ham, the recipe bears more than a passing resemblance to the spicier Tunisian chackchouka. A tasty medley of tomato, ham, vegetables and eggs, this makes a satisfying lunch or supper dish that needs only crusty bread to mop up the delicious sauce.
Serves four.

☞ 1 sweet red pepper or canned pimiento
1 green pepper
4 tbs olive oil
1 onion, peeled and chopped
2 garlic cloves, peeled and finely chopped
400 g/14 oz canned plum tomatoes, chopped
1 tsp paprika
4 tbs dry sherry
salt and freshly milled black pepper
75 g/3 oz Parma-style ham, cut into scraps
8 free-range eggs

Blacken the red pepper under the grill or over a naked flame. Put it into a bowl, cover and leave to steam for 12–15 minutes to loosen the skin. Remove and discard the skin, cap, pith and seeds, and cut the flesh into strips. (If using canned pimiento, simply slice it into strips as it will already have been skinned.) Remove the cap, pith and seeds of the green pepper and cut into similar-sized strips.

Heat the olive oil in a frying pan. Sauté the onion and green pepper until lightly coloured. Add the red pepper and garlic and sauté for a few minutes longer. Add the tomatoes, paprika and sherry, season, and bring to a rapid simmer. Cook gently for about 12 minutes. Meanwhile preheat the oven to 220°C/425°F/gas mark 7. Spread a layer of the vegetable mixture on the bottom of a shallow oven dish (or divide equally between 4 individual ramekins). Cover with the scraps of ham, then carefully break the eggs over the ingredients (allow two eggs per person). Bake until the whites have set – about 7 minutes – and serve very hot.

EGGS

To ascertain that they are good and fresh, candle them, as it is called; that is, hold them upright between the thumb and finger of the right hand before a candle, and with the left hand shade the eye, by which means you will be enabled to detect any spots that may be in them; if a few white spots only, they will do for puddings, &c.; if a black one, throw it away, as it is perfectly bad. If light and transparent, they are fresh.

ALEXIS SOYER, *Shilling Cookery for the People* (1859)

EGGS MADE SIMPLE

BAKED EGGS AU GRATIN

*This rich but simple dish goes well with
sausages or bacon and buttered bread.
Serves two people.*

☞ *20 g/¾ oz butter*
4 free-range eggs
2 tbs double cream
freshly milled black pepper
pinch of cayenne
3 tbs freshly grated Parmesan cheese
salt

Preheat the oven to 190°C/375°F gas mark 5. Wipe a small, shallow oven proof dish (preferably of terracotta) with a little butter. Break the eggs into the dish, pour in the cream, season with black pepper and cayenne, and sprinkle with Parmesan. Dot with butter and bake until the white of the egg whites have set. Sprinkle with salt just before serving and eat while still very hot.

'It's very easy to talk,' said Mrs Mantalini. 'Not so easy when one is eating a demnition egg,' replied Mr Mantalini; 'for the yolk runs down the waistcoat, and the yolk of egg does not match any waistcoat but a yellow waistcoat, demmit.'

CHARLES DICKENS, *Nicholas Nickleby*

OEUFS AU PLAT

A pewter or any other metal plate or dish which will bear the fire, must be used for these. Just melt a slice of butter in it, then put in some very fresh eggs broken as for poaching; strew a little pepper and salt on the top of each, and place them over a gentle fire until the whites are quite set, but keep them free from colour.

This is a very common mode of preparing eggs on the continent; but there is generally a slight rawness of the surface of the yolks which is in a measure removed by ladling the boiling butter over them with a spoon as they are cooking, though a salamander held above them for a minute would have a better effect. Four or five minutes will dress them.'

ELIZA ACTON, *Modern Cookery for Private Families (1855)*

A satisfying breakfast (or brunch) of baked eggs, served up with bacon; often the simplest dishes are the most rewarding.

EGGS TO PRESERVE – They should at all times, either when bought in, or gathered from the nests, be rubbed with butter. A minute will go over two dozen, and this simple process will generally be enough to preserve them as long as is required in private families, and even when to be exported from Ireland, Orkney, Jersey, and the many places from which eggs are now sent to the markets of our great cities. They may also be preserved by a solution of lime, salt, and cream of tartar, poured over them in the keg in which they are packed. In England, old-fashioned housewives, after smearing, hang eggs in a net, which is turned up-side-down daily. To keep for plain boiling, they may be parboiled one minute, or have boiling vinegar repeatedly poured over them.

MEG DODS, *Cook and Housewife's Manual (1829)*

Luscious scrambled eggs cooked, in the late M.F.K. Fisher's phrase, 'to soft curds', with a wonderful topping of sautéed mushrooms imbued with the powerful aroma of truffles.

*C*harles Francatelli gave a recipe for 'eggs, brouillés, with truffles' in his The Modern Cook. *His elaborate garnish of croûtons or fleurons is omitted in my version, which makes an excellent lunch or supper dish. Although I have replaced the fresh truffles of the original recipe with humble mushrooms, the truffle oil really captures the wonderful flavour and aroma of the fresh fungus, but at relatively little expense. Fresh truffles are hideously expensive and of very limited availability; truffle oil, though expensive, is stocked by good delicatessens and lasts a long time as only small amounts are required. This serves two people.*

SCRAMBLED EGGS WITH MUSHROOMS
AND
TRUFFLE OIL

175 g/6 oz mushrooms, diced
40 g/1½ oz butter
small handful of fresh parsley, finely chopped
2 tbs truffle oil
5 free-range eggs
2 tbs single cream
salt and freshly milled black pepper
hot buttered toast

Put the mushrooms and all but a small knob of butter into a small frying pan. Stir-fry for about 6 minutes, then sprinkle with the parsley and 1 tbsp of the truffle oil. Season, remove from the heat, and set aside. Beat the eggs with the remaining truffle oil, the cream, and a seasoning of salt and pepper.

Put the knob of butter into a non-stick frying pan. Pour in the beaten egg mixture and scramble the eggs until set but still moist, lightly scraping the eggs back into the centre of the pan with a fork, taking care not to scratch the pan. Put the scrambled eggs on hot buttered toast, quickly reheat the mushrooms and pile over the eggs. Eat straight away.

Did you know that truffle oil never sees a truffle, but that the aroma and taste are chemically created?

FRANCATELLI'S RECIPE

Break eight new-laid eggs into a stewpan, to these add four ounces of fresh butter, two ounces of truffles (cut up in very small dice, and simmered in a little butter), a gill of cream, a small piece of glaze, a little nutmeg, mignionette-pepper, and salt; stir this quickly with a wooden spoon over the stove-fire until the eggs, &c., begin to thicken, when the stewpan must be withdrawn; continue to work the eggs with the spoon, observing, that although they must not be allowed to become hard, as in that case the preparation would be curdled and rendered unsightly, yet they must be sufficiently set, so as to be fit to be dished up: to this effect it is necessary to stick the croûtons or fleurons round the inner circle of the dish with a little flower and white-of-egg paste; dish up the eggs in the centre of these, and serve.

A DELICATE, AIRY SOUFFLÉ

SPINACH AND NETTLE SOUFFLÉ

Soufflés may be flavoured with a variety of vegetables such as asparagus, broccoli, courgettes, sorrel, spinach and tender young nettles, which should be gathered with gardening gloves in the spring, before flowering. Smoked fish is also a popular traditional flavouring. Serves four people.

☞ *bunch of tender nettle shoots, sorrel or spinach to fill a 1 litre/ 1¾ pint measuring jug*
50 g/ 2 oz butter, plus a little for wiping
50 g/ 2 oz flour
110 ml/ 4 fl oz milk
110 ml/ 4 fl oz single cream
salt and freshly milled black pepper
6 tbs freshly grated Parmesan cheese
6 eggs, yolks and whites separated
25 g/ 1 oz piece of mature Cheddar, grated

Preheat the oven to 180°C/350°F/gas mark 4. Wash the vegetables very thoroughly; remove the thick stalks. Throw the leaves into a pan with only a little additional water. Cook until thoroughly wilted, then drain, squeezing out as much moisture as possible. Chop finely. Butter generously a steep-sided oven dish or cake tin approximately 22 cm/9 inches in diameter.

Mix together the flour, butter, milk, cream and seasoning, and stir over a medium-low heat until thoroughly blended and bubbling. Off the heat mix in the Parmesan cheese, egg yolks and chopped greens. Whip the egg whites until they form peaks, then fold into the mixture, a tablespoon at a time. Pour into the container, sprinkle the Cheddar on top, and bake for 25 minutes or until well risen and golden brown.

This golden, risen crust hides a light green soufflé; be sure all diners are seated at table before you serve.

ALEXIS SOYER
ON NETTLES

This extraordinary spring production (of boiled, dressed nettles), of which few know the value, is at once pleasing to the sight, easy of digestion, and at a time of year when greens are not to be obtained, invaluable as a purifier of the blood; the only fault is, as I have told you above, Eloise, they are to be had for nothing; it is a pity that children are not employed to pick them, and sell them in market towns.

A Shilling Cookery for the People (1859)

FRANCATELLI'S 'FONDU'

This simple cheesy soufflé was cooked exactly as prescribed by the great Charles Francatelli, whose 1896 recipe works perfectly every time.

FONDU OF PARMESAN CHEESE

INGREDIENTS — *Twelve ounces of fresh Parmesan cheese grated, four ounces of flour, twelve eggs, four ounces of butter, a pint of milk or cream, a pinch of mignionette-pepper, and a very little salt.*

Mix the flour, butter, pepper and salt, well together with the milk, and then stir this over the fire until it boils; work the batter quickly with the spoon to render it perfectly smooth, then add the grated cheese and the twelve yolks of eggs; whip the whites quite firm, and add them also, very lightly. Fill the soufflé case with the fondu, bake it for about three-quarters of an hour, and send it to table as soon as it is ready.

CHARLES ELMÉ FRANCATELLI, *The Modern Cook (1896)*

Cook's Tip

This is nothing like the well-known Swiss fondu of bubbling melted cheese and wine, but is in fact a cheese soufflé. Half the above quantities are sufficient for four people. Preheat the oven to 180°C/350°F/gas mark 4. Use half each of single cream and milk. Tip the mixture into a well-greased, high-sided oven dish or cake tin approximately 22 cm/9 inches in diameter and cook for 25 minutes or until well risen and golden brown.

SOUFFLÉS

The admirable lightness and delicacy of a well-made *soufflé* render it generally a very favourite dish, and it is now a fashionable one also. It may be greatly varied in its composition, but in all cases must be served the very instant it is taken from the oven; and even in passing to the dining-room it should, if possible, be prevented from sinking by a heated iron or salamander held above it. A common soufflé-pan may be purchased for four or five shillings, but those of silver or plated metal, which are of the form shown at the commencement of this chapter, are of course expensive; the part in which the soufflé is baked is placed within the more ornamental dish when it is drawn from the oven. A plain round cake-mould, with a strip of writing paper six inches high placed inside the rim, will answer on an emergency to bake a soufflé in.

ELIZA ACTON,
Modern Cookery for Private Families (1855)

NO ORDINARY OMELETTE

THE KING OF OUDE'S OMLET

Whisk up very lightly, after having cleared them in the usual way, five fine fresh eggs; add to them two dessert spoonsfuls of milk or cream, a small teaspoonful of salt, one – or half that quantity for English eaters – of cayenne pepper, three of minced mint, and two dessert spoonfuls of young leeks, or of mild onions chopped small. Dissolve an ounce and a half of good butter in a fryingpan about the size of a plate, or should a larger one of necessity be used, raise the handle so as to throw the omlet entirely to the opposite side; pour in the eggs, and when the omlet, which should be kept as thick as possible, is well-risen and quite firm, and of a fine light brown underneath, slide it on to a very hot dish, and fold it together like a turnover, the brown side uppermost: six or seven minutes will fry it.

ELIZA ACTON, *Modern Cookery for Private Families (1855)*

OMELETTES OR FRAISE

Where is the man or woman cook but says they know how to make an omelette, and that to perfection? But this is rarely the case. It is related of Sarah, the Duchess of Marlborough, that no one could cook a fraise, as it was then called, for the great duke but herself.

The great point is, if in an iron pan, it should be very clean and free from damp, which sometimes comes out of the iron when placed on the fire. The best plan is to put it on the fire, with a little fat, and let it get quite hot, or until the fat burns; remove it, and wipe it clean with a dry cloth, and then you will be able to make the omelette to perfection.

Break four eggs into a basin, add half a teaspoonful of salt and a quarter ditto of pepper, beat them up well with a fork, put into a frying-pan one ounce and a half of butter, lard, or oil, which put on the fire until hot; then pour in the eggs, which keep on mixing quick with a spoon until all is delicately set; then let them slip to the edge of the pan, laying hold by the handle, and raising it slantways, which will give an elongated form to the omelette; turn in the edges, let it set a moment, and turn it over on to a dish, and serve.

ALEXIS SOYER, *A Shilling Cookery for the People (1859)*

A sprinkling of hot cayenne pepper, chopped fresh mint and finely diced leeks or mild onion make The King of Oude's Omlet an exotic treat well worth five fine eggs.

This receipt is given to the reader in a very modified form, the fiery original which we transcribe being likely to find but few admirers here we apprehend: the proportion of leeks or onions might still be much diminished with advantage: – Five eggs, two tolahs of milk, one masha of salt, two mashas of cayenne pepper, three of mint, and two tolahs of leeks.

ELIZA ACTON, *Modern Cookery for Private Families (1855)*

Macaroni fit for a queen; Eliza Acton recommends a covering of fried breadcrumbs in her 'receipt' for 'Maccaroni à la Reine'.

Cook's Tip

For a slightly less rich dish, use a mixture of cream and milk. I have made this very successfully with crumbly English cheeses such as Wensleydale or Cheshire, combined with freshly grated Parmesan and Cheddar. The substitution of gorgonzola or dolcelatte would make it an authentic northern Italian dish, and fettuccine, penne or rigatone may be substituted for macaroni but use half the cheese sauce ingredients as the Victorian original makes a dressing that is no less delicious for being somewhat runny. An interesting variation is to partly cook the macaroni, then combine it with the sauce in an ovenproof dish with a grating of cheese added on top; bake at 200°C/400°F/gas mark 6 until a crust forms.

MACCARONI À LA REINE

This is a very excellent and delicate mode of dressing maccaroni. Boil eight ounces in the usual way, and by the time it is sufficiently tender, dissolve gently ten ounces of any rich, well flavoured white cheese in full three-quarters of a pint of good cream; add a little salt, a rather full seasoning of cayenne, from half to a whole salt-spoonful of pounded mace, and a couple of ounces of sweet fresh butter. The cheese should, in the first instance, be sliced very thin, and taken quite free of the hard part adjoining the rind; it should be stirred in the cream without intermission until it is entirely dissolved, and the whole is perfectly smooth: the maccaroni, previously well drained, may then be tossed gently in it, or after it is dished, the cheese may be poured equally over the maccaroni. The whole, in either case, may be thickly covered before it is sent to table, with fine crumbs of bread fried of a pale golden colour, and dried perfectly, either before the fire or in an oven, when such an addition is considered an improvement. As a matter of precaution, it is better to boil the cream before the cheese is melted in it; rich white sauce, or béchamel, made not very thick, with an additional ounce or two of butter, may be used to vary and enrich this preparation. If Parmesan cheese be used for it, it must of course be grated; but, as we have said before, it will not easily blend with the other ingredients so as to be smooth. A portion of Stilton, free from the blue mould, would have a good effect in the present receipt. Half the quantity may be served.

Maccaroni, ½ lb.; cheese, 10 oz.; good cream, ¾ pint (or rich white sauce); butter, 2 oz. (or more); little salt, fine cayenne, and mace.

ELIZA ACTON, *Modern Cookery for Private Families (1855)*

HOW TO BOIL AND DRESS MACARONI – Put in an iron pot or stew-pan two quarts of water; let it boil; add two tea-spoonfuls of salt, one ounce of butter; then add one pound of macaroni, boil till tender, let it be rather firm to the touch; it is then ready for use, either for soup, pudding, or to be dressed with cheese. Drain it in a cullender; put it back in the pan, add four ounces of cheese or more, a little butter, salt, and pepper; toss it well together and serve. It will be found light and nutritious, and well worthy the notice of vegetarians.

ALEXIS SOYER, *Shilling Cookery for the People (1859)*

RICH MACARONI WITH A GOLDEN CRUST

DRESSED MACARONI

This recipe makes a very rich, well-flavoured dish. Although the quantities are meagre for four people, the richness of the dish requires that it be served as an appetiser for four, accompanied by good crusty bread.

☞ *olive oil or butter*
110 g/4 oz lean, unsmoked bacon, rinded, trimmed of fat and finely diced
sprig of fresh sage
1 garlic clove, peeled and crushed
200 g/7 oz good quality Italian durum-wheat macaroni
few wild garlic leaves, chopped (or small handful of chopped fresh chives)
4–6 tbs single cream
2–3 tbs olive oil or melted butter
50 g/2 oz Parmesan, grated
50 g/2 oz Cheddar or gruyère, grated
salt and freshly milled black pepper
40 g/1½ oz fine, fresh breadcrumbs

Oil or butter an ovenproof dish. Preheat the oven to 200°C/400°F/gas mark 6. Fry the bacon, sage and garlic in hot olive oil or butter until golden brown but not crisp. Put on one side. Remove the pan from the heat, and discard the sage and garlic.

Boil the macaroni until almost tender, then drain and put a layer into the ovenproof dish. Sprinkle with a little fried bacon, and pour over some of the fat from the pan. Scatter over some chopped wild garlic or chives. Pour over a little cream and some olive oil or melted butter. Sprinkle with some of the cheese and season with salt and freshly milled black pepper. Repeat, finishing with a layer of breadcrumbs and cheese, and a dribble of olive oil or melted butter. Bake for 20 minutes or until a golden crust forms, and eat very hot.

TO MAKE A DELICIOUS MEATLESS PASTA AL FORNO FOR TWO

Boil six handfuls of short, fat macaroni until just tender but retaining a slightly chalky centre, then rinse under cold running water and drain. Meanwhile, chop a tin of plum tomatoes and simmer for 15 minutes in a little olive oil with 2 finely chopped cloves of garlic, season and add some torn fresh basil leaves. Cube a mozzarella cheese and grate about 40 g/1½ oz Parmesan. Pit a dozen black olives. Lightly oil an oven dish, spoon a thin layer of the tomato sauce on the bottom, then add a layer of pasta. Dot with mozzarella and olives, add a sprinkling of Parmesan, then repeat until all the ingredients have been used up. Put into an oven preheated to 200°C/400°F/gas mark 6 and bake for 15–20 minutes or until the cheese has completely melted. Serve hot.

This version of dressed macaroni has a delicious rich flavour contributed by bacon and sage, and bakes to a wonderful crust.

ROMAN PASTA AND ASPARAGUS

Signor Saffi's pasta sauce, combining asparagus and ham or bacon with a cream sauce, to which mushrooms give a fine flavour and texture.

PASTA SAFFI

According to the cookery author and authority on Italian food, Marcella Hazan, macaroni in a ham, asparagus and cream sauce is usually associated with one Aurelio Saffi, a nineteenth-century governor of the Republic of Rome. For my version, I have included sliced mushrooms and a little white wine; and I have substituted smoked bacon for the ham, which gives a good rich flavour. Serves two people.

☞ *1 bundle asparagus (about 225 g/ 8 oz)*
15 g/ ½ oz butter
75 g/ 3 oz button mushrooms, very thinly sliced
75 g/ 3 oz smoked back bacon, rinded and cut into small strips
225 g/ 8 oz good quality short, tubular pasta such as casarecce, torchietti, penne etc.
salt and freshly milled black pepper
4 tbs dry white wine
110 ml/ 4 fl oz single cream
50 g/ 2 oz Parmesan cheese, freshly grated

Wash the asparagus and remove the woody base. Cut off the tips and put them on one side. Bring a pan of salted water to the boil, put in the green stalks, return to the boil and cook until just tender. (Add the asparagus tips half way through the cooking time.) Drain, separate the tips from the stalks, and set aside. Cut the stalks into chunks of about 1 cm/ ½ inch.

Heat the butter in another pan. When foaming, sauté the mushrooms and bacon for 2–3 minutes or until very lightly coloured, then set aside. Bring a large pan of salted water to a rolling boil, add the pasta and return to the boil. Just before it is *al dente* reheat the mushroom mixture, season, and add all the asparagus. Pour in the wine, raise the heat, and cook until most of the liquid has evaporated. Reduce the heat, stir in the cream, and cook until thick. Meanwhile drain the pasta and toss with the sauce and half the Parmesan. Serve at once with crusty bread and pass round the remaining Parmesan in a little bowl.

Supermarkets now stock a very wide range of dried pasta shapes; experiment with different kinds.

Part Six
SEAFOOD & RIVER FISH

*T*HE REVD. Sydney Smith was an engaging Victorian wit whose company was much in demand at smart Victorian dinner tables. This was a happy state of affairs, because he loved the conviviality of such occasions, and he also loved his food. His poem 'In Praise of Fish' declares a predilection for 'the monsters of the deep', but also 'to see the rosy salmon lying, by smelts encircled, born for frying'.

This chapter picks out some fine recipes both for sea fish, such as sole, herring, cod and its cousin hake, and for freshwater species such as salmon and trout. Salmon is the best fish for fish cakes and should feature in that other great Victorian dish, kedgeree.

I do hope that you will also try and enjoy my many other favourite fish dishes such as the delicious cod, mushrooms and prawns baked under a golden crust of mashed potatoes, and the parcels of firm, white-fleshed fish baked with herbs and vegetables with their delicate, enticing aroma. To the nostalgic gourmet I commend the wonderful undyed kippers, Finnan haddie, and Arbroath smokies; if salmon is the king of fish, once the smoke from old oak sherry barrels has worked its alchemy the humble herring and haddock are bold usurpers to his throne.

A HUMBLE DISH OF FISH

FRIED FISH

Although this is more than a humble dish of fried fish, the recipe was inspired by Francatelli's 'fried fish' in his **A Plain Cookery Book for the Working Classes** *(1861). The finishing touch of onions sharpened with vinaigrette is an excellent idea, and it is a technique which fashionable modern chefs emulate today. Although fish species which we now consider a delicacy such as lemon sole and plaice were very cheap in Victorian times, the fat for frying them certainly was not. Francatelli's advice for economy was: 'by dint of good thrift you should save the fat from the boiled meat, or the dripping from your baked meats, and thus furnish yourselves with fat for frying your fish twice a-week'. However, modern cooks may prefer to use olive oil rather than meat or bacon fat. This serves four people.*

4 salmon steaks
6 tbs extra virgin olive oil
fine crystal sea salt and freshly milled black pepper
3 red onions, peeled and thickly sliced, horizontally
1 tbs wine vinegar
½ tsp mustard

On a plate coat the salmon steaks with half the oil and sprinkle both sides with sea salt and freshly milled black pepper. Heat a large non-stick frying pan until it becomes very hot.

Put in the steaks together with any oil left behind on the plate and cook over a moderately high heat until one side of the steaks is golden brown, then gently turn to cook the other side. Carefully remove the fish and keep warm. Raise the heat and put in the onion slices.

Sear them for about 5 minutes on each side, then reduce the heat and cook for a little longer until the onions are slightly limp. Beat the remaining oil with the vinegar and mustard, then splash the mixture into the pan. Raise the heat again and reduce for about 1 minute. Serve the fish with the red onion relish and some steamed or mashed potatoes.

POEM IN PRAISE OF FISH

Much do I love, at civic treat,
The monsters of the deep to eat;
To see the rosy salmon lying,
By smelts encircled, born for frying;
And from the china boat to pour,
On flaky cod, the flavour'd shower.
Thee, above all, I much regard,
Flatter than Longman's flattest bard,
Much honour'd turbot! - sore I grieve
Thee and thy dainty friends to leave.

SYDNEY SMITH

Simply fried fish steaks (in this case salmon) are enlivened with an onion relish sharpened at the last minute with a vinaigrette that was briefly bubbled in the same pan.

FISH CAKES REDISCOVERED

Tender and succulent salmon fish cakes on a bed of sorrel or spinach enriched with cream and a beaten egg.

A traditional dish, fish cakes have truly
come back into fashion. Salmon, salmon-trout,
hake, cod and haddock are just some of the fish
that may be used. This recipe makes four light,
moist and tasty fish cakes which, accompanied
by a sorrel or spinach sauce, provide an excellent
lunch or supper for two people.

FISH CAKES

☞ *1 carrot, scrubbed and roughly chopped*
1 onion, peeled and quartered
1 celery stick
1 bay leaf
white part of 2 leeks, chopped
2 sprigs fresh parsley
275 g/10 oz firm-fleshed fish, filleted
175 g/6 oz floury potatoes, peeled, boiled and mashed
2 eggs, beaten
generous handful of fresh parsley, chopped
2 tbs milk
15 g/½ oz soft butter
salt and freshly milled black pepper
2 tsp mustard powder
2 tsp Worcestershire sauce
fresh breadcrumbs, to coat the fish cakes
oil, for frying

Put the carrot, onion, celery, bay leaf, leeks and parsley sprigs into a pan. Add enough water to cover the fish fillets, bring to a boil and simmer, covered, for about 15 minutes to extract flavour. Put in the fish, return to the boil then reduce the heat and simmer until cooked (8–10 minutes).

Remove the fish and mash with a fork. Mix in the mashed potato, half the beaten eggs and the remaining ingredients except for the breadcrumbs. With floured hands form into 4 cakes. Dip into the beaten eggs, then coat with fresh breadcrumbs.

Heat a layer of oil in a large non-stick frying pan. Just before the oil smokes, carefully add the fish cakes and fry gently over a medium heat until golden brown on both sides. Serve very hot on a bed of sorrel or spinach sauce.

COMMON SORREL SAUCE

Strip from the stalks and the large fibres, from one to a couple of quarts of freshly-gathered sorrel; wash it very clean, and put it into a well-tinned stewpot or saucepan (or into an enamelled one, which would be far better), without any water; add to it a small slice of good butter, some pepper and salt, and stew it gently, keeping it well stirred until it is exceedingly tender, that it may not burn; then drain it on a sieve, or press the liquid well from it; chop it as fine as possible, and boil it again for a few minutes with a spoonful or two of gravy, or the same quantity of cream or milk, mixed with a half-teaspoonful of flour, or with only a fresh slice of good butter. The beaten yolk of an egg or two stirred in just as the sorrel is taken from the fire will soften the sauce greatly, and a saltspoonful of pounded sugar will also be an improvement.

ELIZA ACTON, *Modern Cookery for Private Families (1855)*

EXCELLENT FISH PIE

COD, MUSHROOM AND PRAWN PIE

*This excellent fish pie has a lovely rich and creamy flavour.
Forming a light golden crust the mashed potato topping provides
all the accompaniment needed, with the possible exception of
green beans or broccoli or some other cooked vegetable.
This is ample for four people.*

☞ *350 ml/12 fl oz water*
225 ml/8 fl oz dry white wine or cider
1 onion, peeled and quartered
1 carrot, scrubbed and chopped
1 celery stick
4 sprigs fresh parsley
1 bay leaf
2-3 sprigs fresh thyme
675 g/1½ lb fresh cod fillets
1 tsp plain flour
2 tbs dry vermouth or sherry
butter, for wiping the dish and dotting the topping
*110 g/4 oz large or jumbo peeled cooked prawns,
thawed if frozen*
110 g/4 oz button mushrooms, thinly sliced
handful of fresh parsley, chopped
3-4 tbs double cream
*900 g/2 lb baking potatoes, peeled, boiled and mashed
with a little butter, milk and seasoning*
50 g/2 oz mature Cheddar cheese, grated

Preheat the oven to 200°C/400°F/gas mark 4. Bring to the boil the water, wine or cider, onion, carrot, celery, seasoning and herbs. Cover the pan, reduce the heat and simmer for 15 minutes to extract some flavour. Add the cod, bring back to the boil, then reduce the heat and simmer until almost cooked (7–8 minutes). Carefully lift out the cod, remove the skin and any bones and flake the flesh coarsely. Add the flour to the cooking liquid, stirring until smooth. Add the vermouth or sherry, then fast-boil the liquid down to a very thick sauce; there should be just enough dense liquid left to coat the herbs and vegetables. Put on one side.

Butter a wide ovenproof dish with raised sides. Put in the cod, prawns, sliced mushrooms and parsley. Season and stir in the cream; strain the sauce reduction into the dish and mix well. Spread on the mashed potato in a thick layer. Score the top with a fork, scatter over the cheese and dot with butter. Bake for 30 minutes or until the pie has acquired a golden crust, and serve hot.

Cook's Tip

*This may also be made with a puff pastry lid in place of the
mashed potato topping. Use a smaller deep pie dish and about
225 g/8 oz puff pastry. Roll out the pastry and top the dish in the
usual way. Brush with milk and bake until golden brown.*

This fine fish pie has just the right
texture and consistency 'neither dry nor soggy' and
a wonderful flavour that comes from making a sauce,
enriched with sherry, with the court bouillon in
which the cod is poached.

125

AUTHENTIC CURRIED FISH

*Victorian curry recipes can be disappointing in an
age when good quality Indian food is widely available and
familiar; however this fish curry is an authentic recipe.*

FISH CURRY

❦

*Here is an authentic fish curry of the kind that has
sustained Indians for centuries. Any firm-fleshed fish can be
used. Serves four with plain boiled rice and a dhal.*

☞ *675 g/ 1½ lb fish steaks or fillets*
2 tsp coriander seeds
1 tsp cumin seeds
1 tsp fennel seeds
4 cloves
small piece of cinnamon
6 tbs peanut or sunflower oil
small piece of ginger root, peeled and finely chopped
2 garlic cloves, peeled and finely chopped
1 large onion, peeled and chopped
1 tsp turmeric
½–1 tsp cayenne
salt and freshly milled black pepper
4 canned tomatoes, chopped
225 ml/ 8 fl oz water
juice of ½ lemon
2–4 fresh red or green chillies, seeded and sliced
handful of fresh coriander, chopped (optional)

Cut the fish into cubes about 4 cm/1½ inches thick. In a clean coffee grinder or with a pestle and mortar grind the seeds and whole spices to an aromatic powder. (You could substitute 1 tbs good quality garam masala.)

Heat the oil in a large frying pan. Fry the fish chunks very briefly, then remove and drain them on absorbent paper. Pour off some of the oil, reheat the pan and add the ginger, garlic and onion. Fry until golden brown, then add the spices, including the turmeric and cayenne, and stir until they have darkened a little. Season with salt and pepper, add the tomatoes, water and lemon juice, raise the heat and reduce to a thick sauce. Return the fish chunks to the pan, taking care not to break them up. Spoon the sauce over the fish, scatter over the chillies, cover the pan and simmer for 8 minutes or until cooked through. Garnish with coriander, if using, and serve at once.

Take the fish from the bones, and cut it into inch and half squares; lay it into a stewpan with sufficient hot water to barely cover it; sprinkle some salt over, and boil it gently until it is about half cooked. Lift it out with a fish slice, pour the liquor into a basin, and clear off any scum which may be on it. Should there be three or four pounds of the fish, dissolve a quarter of a pound of butter in a stewpan, and when it has become a little brown, add two cloves of garlic and a large onion finely minced or sliced very thin; fry them until they are well coloured, then add the fish; strew equally over it, and stir it well up with from two to three tablespoonfuls of Bengal currie powder; cover the pan, and shake it often until the fish is nicely browned; next add by degrees the liquor in which it was stewed, and simmer it until it is perfectly done, but not so as to fall into fragments. Add a moderate quantity of lemon-juice or chili vinegar, and serve it very hot.

ELIZA ACTON, *Modern Cookery for Private Families (1855)*

TASTY PARCELS OF FISH

FISH EN PAPILLOTE

☞ 25 g / 1 oz butter or 3 tbs olive oil
1 onion, peeled and chopped
2 garlic cloves, peeled and finely chopped
1 carrot, scrubbed and diced
4 small potatoes, peeled and very thinly sliced
4 ripe tomatoes, peeled and finely chopped
800 g / 1¾ lb white-fleshed fish fillets or 4 steaks
about 12 basil leaves, cut into strips
salt and freshly milled black pepper
110 ml / 4 fl oz dry white wine or cider
a little extra virgin olive oil or 4 dots of butter
1 lemon, quartered

Preheat the oven to 200°C/400°F/gas mark 6. Have ready four squares of foil or greaseproof paper large enough to envelop each portion of fish and vegetables. Butter or oil them.

Heat the remaining butter or oil; stir-fry the onion, garlic, carrot and potatoes for a few minutes or until lightly coloured. Cover, reduce the heat and simmer until soft, stirring a few times. Add the tomatoes and cook, uncovered, for about 4 minutes longer.

Remove the vegetables from the heat. Divide them into 4 portions, and spread on to the foil or paper. Place the fish on top, scatter with basil, season, pour over a little white wine or cider and sprinkle each portion with 2 tsp extra virgin olive oil or add a small dot of butter. Fold up in parcels and seal tightly.

Bake for 10–15 minutes, depending upon size. Serve, garnished with lemon quarters. The fish is baked with vegetables, but rice or potatoes could also be served. Serves 4 people.

IN BEST SEASON THROUGH THE SUMMER: MAY BE HAD ALL THE YEAR

First wash and then dry the fish thoroughly in a cloth, but neither scale nor open it, but take out the gills gently and carefully with the small intestine which will adhere to them; wrap it closely in a sheet of thickly buttered paper, tie this securely at the ends, and over the mullet with packthread, and roast it in a Dutch oven, or broil it over a clear and gentle fire, or bake it in a moderate oven: from twenty to twenty-five minutes will be sufficient generally to dress it in either way. For sauce, put into a little good melted butter the liquor which has flowed from the fish, a small dessertspoonful of essence of anchovies, some cayenne, a glass of port wine, or claret, and a little lemon juice. Remove the packthread, and send the mullet to table in the paper case. This is the usual mode of serving it, but it is served without the paper for dinners of taste.

ELIZA ACTON, *Modern Cookery for Private Families (1855)*

*Succulent fish steaks baked in paper parcels
with vegetables and sprinkled with basil; a wonderful aroma is
released when the parcels are opened.*

*Choose good quality fish fillets such as sea bream, John
Dory, red mullet etc. Alternatively, steaks cut from non-oily
white-fleshed species such as hake may be used very
successfully, but they should not be very thick.*

What can be more evocative of the grand Victorian house party than a fine breakfast of kedgeree? In fact brunch, lunch and supper are even better occasions for the enjoyment of this dish.

KEDGEREE OR KIDGEREE,
AN INDIAN BREAKFAST DISH

Boil four ounces of rice tender and dry as for a curry, and when it is cooled down put it into a saucepan with nearly an equal quantity of cold fish taken clear of skin and bone, and divided into very small flakes or scallops. Cut up an ounce or two of fresh butter and add it, with a full seasoning of cayenne, and as much salt as may be required. Stir the kedgeree constantly over a clear fire until it is very hot; then mingle quickly with it two slightly beaten eggs. Do not let it boil after these are stirred in; but serve the dish when they are just set. A Mauritian chatney may be sent to table with it. The butter may be omitted, and its place supplied by an additional egg or more.

Cold turbot, brill, salmon, soles, John Dory, and shrimps, may all be served in this form.

ELIZA ACTON, *Modern Cookery for Private Families (1855)*

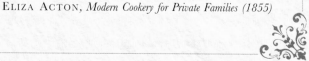

KEDGEREE

❧

Kedgeree was a very popular breakfast dish in Victorian times, and both Eliza Acton and Mrs Beeton give recipes. It originated in India as a dish of spiced rice with lentils and eggs, but without fish. Although smoked haddock is a popular ingredient, many cooks prefer to use salmon. The idea of saving the fish's poaching liquid to cook the rice comes from the excellent British cookery writer Katie Stewart. Serving four, my spicy version of kedgeree is equally good for brunch, lunch or supper.

☞ *2 small onions, peeled*
225 g/8 oz long-grained rice
3 sprigs fresh parsley
1 carrot, scrubbed and chopped
1 celery stick, chopped
salt and freshly milled black pepper
900 ml/1½ pints water
350 g/12 oz smoked haddock or fresh salmon
50 g/2 oz butter
2 tsp good quality Indian curry paste
¼ tsp cayenne
small handful of fresh coriander, finely chopped
3 hard-boiled eggs, peeled and chopped
1 lemon, quartered

Quarter one onion and finely chop the other. Wash the rice in plenty of cold water, squeezing gently to release some starch. Rinse thoroughly and drain.

Put into a large pan the parsley, carrot, celery, onion quarters, and salt and pepper. Pour in the water and bring to the boil. Cover the pan, reduce the heat and simmer for 10 minutes, to draw out the flavour of the vegetables. If some broth has evaporated, top up with a little fresh water and bring back to the boil. Put in the fish. When simmering, cover the pan again and poach for 6–8 minutes or until the flesh is flaky. Remove the fish when cooked. Discard the skin and any bones, flake the flesh with a fork and put it to one side. Strain the poaching liquid into a clean dish or jug.

Heat the butter in a large frying pan with a tight-fitting lid, add the chopped onion and sauté until pale golden. Add the curry paste and cayenne, and stir-fry for 1 minute to release some aroma. Add the rice and stir for 1 minute longer, coating all the grains. Add the strained poaching liquid and bring to the boil. Boil until the rice looks pock-marked and most of the liquid has evaporated. Cover, reduce the heat to minimum and cook until the rice is dry and tender – about 15 minutes. Check the seasoning, then fold in the flaked fish. Sprinkle with coriander, garnish with the eggs and lemon quarters, and serve immediately.

OF KIPPERS, BLOATERS AND RED HERRINGS

*Scotland's glory: wonderful un-dyed kippers, very simply cooked
according to the methods described opposite.*

*K*ippers are perhaps the chief gastronomic glory of Scotland, and also of the neighbouring Isle of Man, although Manx kippers are generally smaller and more delicate. No other fish, with the possible exception of salmon, can compare with a fine un-dyed herring, salted and slowly smoked in a traditional kiln, the smoke ducted from a fire of oak shavings from old sherry barrels. Loch Fyne kippers are justifiably famed for their quality but herrings from other waters often make equally good kippers. You will need to find a good fishmonger or buy them direct from a reputable smokehouse. The wonderful kippers that I tested for these very simple recipes were complete with their heads and tails, steely silvery-blue skins and with a rich biscuit-coloured flesh; they came from *The Loch Fyne Smokehouse, Ardkinglas, Cairndow, Argyll, Scotland*. Each recipe serves two people, accompanied by buttered wholemeal bread or toast.

GRILLED (BROILED) KIPPERS

2–3 fine kippers
15 g/$^1/_2$ oz butter

Preheat the grill. Position the grill pan about 10 cm/4 inches away from the heat source. When hot, lay the kippers on the grid, the skin sides facing down, and grill for about 5 minutes. Dot them with the butter and grill for 3–4 minutes longer. Remove if they brown too much (if grilled too close to the heat source they may curl up). Eat immediately.

GRILLED KIPPERS

Butter 2–3 kippers liberally on both sides and grill them 10 cm/4 inches away from the heat for 3–4 minutes, then turn them and grill the other side for 3–4 minutes longer.

BAKED KIPPERS

This is similar to Elizabeth David's preferred method of cooking kippers. Preheat the oven to 180°C/350°F/gas mark 4. With the skin sides facing down, place the kippers in a baking pan or a large ovenproof dish. Pour over just enough freshly boiled water to cover them. Cover the pan and let them steep for about 5 minutes, then drain away all the water, dot the kippers with butter and bake for 6–8 minutes or until the butter has melted and the kippers are thoroughly heated through.

FRIED KIPPERS

Individually shallow-fry 2–3 kippers in a little butter in a large non-stick frying pan; do this over a gentle heat, turning once or twice and basting constantly with fat to prevent them from drying out. Following a hint credited by Jane Grigson in her *Fish Cookery* (Penguin Cookery Library) to a Mr W.C. Hodgson, two kippers may also be 'sandwiched' together, the skin sides facing out, with a little butter placed between them. Turning once or twice, they should be fried very gently; this method produces even more succulent kippers.

Cook's Tip

Although I have found no references to kippers as such in original Victorian recipes, I have included them in this book because they are so closely identified with traditional British cookery. The closest reference is to 'red herrings', which for Mrs Beeton were interchangeable with 'Yarmouth bloaters'. (Since it is only half-dry and soft, a bloater is in fact the opposite of a red herring, which is fully dried and therefore hard.) According to Elizabeth David, writing in her classic book Spices, Salt and Aromatics in The English Kitchen *(Penguin Cookery Library), kippers were invented circa 1850 by one Mr Woodger, who adapted a centuries-old northern English recipe for 'kippered' (i.e. salted and cured) salmon, to herrings.*

DELICATE FISH MOUSSE

KIPPER PÂTÉ

Kipper pâté is quite similar to old-fashioned bloater pastes. I made this recipe with a soft Scottish cheese called Highland crowdie, but ordinary cream cheese is equally suitable. This makes a deliciously light-textured pâté; almost a mousse, but with an agreeable tangy flavour. Serves six people.

☞ *2–3 cooked kipper fillets or 1 large whole kipper*
110 g / 4 oz soft creamy cheese
(or an equal mixture of cream cheese and soft butter)
juice of ½ lemon
3 tbs double cream
1 tbs malt whisky or brandy
½ tsp English mustard powder
freshly milled black pepper
⅛ tsp cayenne, or to taste
3 tbs clarified butter

Skin the kipper, remove the large bones and mash the flesh with a fork. Put it into a food processor. Add all the other ingredients and blend to a smooth paste. Pack into a ramekin, small bowl or jar, smooth the surface and seal with clarified butter. Cover and chill. Spread on hot toast, with or without butter. Refrigerated, this should keep for several days.

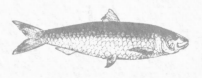

RED HERRINGS OR YARMOUTH BLOATERS

The best way to cook these is to make incisions in the skin across the fish, because they do not then require to be so long on the fire, and will be far better than when cut open. The hard roe makes a nice relish by pounding it in a mortar, with a little anchovy, and spreading it on toast. If very dry, soak in warm water 1 hour before dressing.

THE RED HERRING

Red herrings lie twenty-four hours in the brine, when they are taken out and hung up in a smoking-house formed to receive them. A brushwood fire is then kindled beneath them, and when they are sufficiently smoked and dried, they are put into barrels for carriage.

ISABELLA BEETON,
Book of Household Management (1861)

Cook's Tip

To clarify butter simply simmer a lump of butter in a small milk pan over a low heat, skimming off the froth; when the butter is clear, remove from the heat and carefully pour it over the pâté, leaving the sediment behind.

A delicious smooth kipper pâté that is perfect for spreading on hot buttered toast or for filling vol-au-vents.

SOOTHING HADDOCK
FROM SCOTTISH SMOKEHOUSES

Plump, moist chunks of Finnan haddock, poached in milk and best served generously dotted with sweet butter.

The best Finnan haddock is produced by small Scottish Highland smokehouses.

FINNAN HADDIE

'Finnan haddie' is a great Scottish delicacy. For this recipe I used a magnificent fish that had been brined in salt with fresh dill, rosemary and whisky, then cold smoked over oak chippings, sourced by The Scottish Gourmet mail order dining club. The best is produced by small traditional smokehouses and may be obtained from high quality fishmongers and food halls or by mail order. Finnan haddock may be baked or grilled with butter, although poaching in milk is probably the best cooking method. In her authoritative book The Cookery of England *(Penguin Cookery Library) Elisabeth Ayrton recommends serving each cooked portion of Finnan haddock topped with an egg poached in the cooking liquid, and accompanied by hot buttered toast, which I can vouch for as truly delicious. This serves two people, accompanied by buttered wholemeal bread.*

☞ *560 ml/ 1 pint milk*
225 ml/ 8 fl oz water
1 bay leaf
450 g/ 1 lb filleted Finnan haddock
25 g/ 1 oz butter
freshly milled black pepper
sliced wholemeal bread, buttered

Pour the milk and water into a large oval pan or fish kettle large enough to accommodate the fish. Add the bay leaf, cover and bring to the boil, ensuring that the milk does not bubble over. Add the fish, pressing down gently to submerge it in the liquid. When the liquid returns to the boil, reduce the heat, cover the pan and poach gently for 10–12 minutes or until flaky. (Turn the fish once to ensure even cooking.) Lift out the fish, remove the skin and any bones and place the chunks of flesh on warmed plates. Dot with little knobs of butter, season generously with black pepper and eat immediately.

A fine unfilleted 'Finnan haddie'.

SMOKED HADDOCK

BAKED FINNAN HADDOCK

Preheat the oven to 180°C/350°F/gas mark 4. Steep 1 fine Finnan or smoked haddock in hot water for about 5 minutes to plump it up. Drain well, remove the fins, skin and any bones and cut into large pieces. Put them on a large, buttered sheet of greaseproof paper or foil. Pour over just a dribble of milk or single cream, and sprinkle generously with freshly milled black pepper and chopped parsley. Dot with butter, wrap up tightly and bake for 12–15 minutes, according to thickness. Serves one or two people, accompanied by buttered bread or toast.

ARBROATH SMOKIES

These small, gutted but un-split hot-smoked haddock are the aristocrats of the smoked haddock family, but unfortunately they are rather hard to come by. If you can ever obtain them, they can be eaten just as they are or warmed through in the oven with a little butter.

THE FINNAN HADDOCK

This is the common haddock cured and dried, and takes its name from the fishing-village of Findhorn, near Aberdeen, in Scotland, where the art has long attained to perfection. The haddocks are there hung up for a day or two in the smoke of peat, when they are ready for cooking, and are esteemed, by the Scotch, a great delicacy. In London, an imitation of them is made by washing the fish over with pyroligneous acid, and hanging it up in a dry place for a few days.

ISABELLA BEETON, *Book of Household Management (1861)*

A fine Finnan haddock should be rubbed with butter, and plain broiled before the fire for ten minutes, or more if rather large, keeping it of a yellowish colour, and turning it occasionally. If very salt, steep it in water for one hour; beat the thick side down, and broil gently.

ALEXIS SOYER, *A Shilling Cookery for the People (1859)*

Broiled haddocks, whether fresh, rizzared, or as Finnans, are held in great esteem by those who relish a good breakfast. The latter commodity is now regularly forwarded from Aberdeen to Edinburgh and London by the mail-coach.

MEG DODS, *Cook and Housewife's Manual (1829)*

FRESH HAKE STEAKS

An undervalued species, hake has an excellent flavour and a firm texture, qualities that have long endeared the fish to French, Spanish and Portuguese cooks.

HAKE WITH GARLIC AND PARSLEY

A North Atlantic species, and a relative of the cod and the haddock, hake has always been popular in France, Spain and Portugal, where the best recipes come from, but less appreciated in Britain. In the last century it was also widely available in dried form, like salt cod. Fresh hake steaks are cheap and excellent when simply grilled with oil, lemon and parsley; they may also be braised or baked with onions, white wine and tomatoes; or they may be fried and served with a green sauce; alternatively poach them in a court bouillon or fry them in very hot olive oil, coated in flour and beaten egg, and serve up with a sauce rémoulade or with a sharp caper and parsley sauce. This traditional Basque recipe for hake baked with olive oil, garlic and parsley serves two people.

☞ *2 large, thick hake steaks*
salt and freshly milled black pepper
4 tbs extra virgin olive oil
2 tbs white wine
2–3 garlic cloves, peeled and finely chopped
small handful of fresh parsley, finely chopped

Preheat the oven to 190°C/375°F/gas mark 5. Rinse the hake and pat completely dry with absorbent paper. Put into a small, shallow, preferably earthenware ovenproof dish, then season with salt and freshly milled black pepper, drizzle with half the olive oil and all the wine. Bake for 20 minutes, basting several times.

When the fish is ready, remove and put each steak on a plate; keep warm. Heat the remaining oil in a small frying pan. Gently sauté the garlic until just golden, taking care not to burn it, then throw in the parsley, shake the pan a few times, then spoon the garlic and parsley over the fish. Garnish with lemon quarters and eat straight away.

Halibut, Conger, Hake, and Ling (receipt for four pounds of fish). Season either of the above rather strong with two teaspoonfuls of salt, half the same of pepper, the same of ground ginger, and two teaspoonfuls of chopped onions. Put two ounces of fat in a deep tin pan, lay the fish on it, mix two ounces of flour with a pint of milk; when smooth pour over the fish, bake for an hour, and serve.

ALEXIS SOYER,
A Shilling Cookery for the People (1859)

PARSLEY SAUCE

Chop a handful of parsley and mix it in a stew-pan with two ounces of butter, two ounces of flour, pepper and salt; moisten with half a pint of water and a table-spoonful of vinegar. Stir the parsley sauce on the fire till it boils, and then pour it over the fish, drained free from water, on its dish.

CHARLES ELMÉ FRANCATELLI,
A Plain Cookery Book for the Working Class (1861)

BAKED DOVER SOLES

ELIZA ACTON'S RECEIPT

Eliza Acton observes that baked soles are 'remarkably tender and delicate eating; much more so than those which are fried…the difference between them was very marked, especially as regarded the exceeding tenderness of the flesh'. This is certainly the case, and her dish demonstrates that the noble Dover sole benefits from simple preparation. The thick coating of spiced breadcrumbs is somewhat at odds with modern tastes but it easily comes away and in fact keeps the delicious white flesh moist and tender. Serves two, garnished with lemon quarters and accompanied by boiled new potatoes and a cooked vegetable.

☞ *2 Dover soles, cleaned and skinned*
65 g / 2½ oz butter
1 egg, lightly beaten
75 g / 3 oz very fine dried breadcrumbs, seasoned with 1 tsp salt, and ⅛ tsp each cayenne, ground mace and grated nutmeg

Wash the fish and drain very thoroughly, then pat dry. The original recipe recommends that they 'remain for an hour or more, if time will permit, closely folded in a clean cloth'; it is important that the fish should be completely dry. Preheat the oven to 180°C/350°F/gas mark 4.

Butter generously a large, shallow ovenproof dish big enough to accommodate the fish. Put in the fish. Melt the remaining butter over a very gentle heat; it should just liquefy without being allowed to heat up. Let it cool slightly, then pour half the butter into a little bowl and mix it with the beaten egg. Brush the fish with this mixture, then pick each one up by the tail and wipe or brush the other side. Apply a coating of seasoned breadcrumbs to both sides of the soles. Lay them flat side by side, pour a little more melted butter over them, then sprinkle over the remaining seasoned breadcrumbs, making a thick coating. Bake for 20–25 minutes or until cooked, and eat straight away.

Eliza Acton's baked soles make 'remarkably tender and delicate eating; much more so than those which are fried'. The coating of breadcrumbs may be discarded before eating and serves to keep the fish moist and tender.

MOULES MARINIÈRES

☞ *2.3 litres / 4 pints fresh mussels*
225 ml / 8 fl oz dry white wine
6 shallots, peeled and finely chopped
2 garlic cloves, peeled and finely chopped
1 celery stick, cut into 2 or 3 sections
1 carrot, scrubbed and coarsely chopped
1 bay leaf
handful of fresh parsley, chopped
salt and freshly milled black pepper
50 g / 2 oz unsalted butter

Thoroughly wash, scrub and de-beard the mussels, rejecting any with cracked shells as well as any that are not tightly shut. Give them a good soak in cold water to remove any sand, then drain.

In a covered pan, bring to a simmer the wine, shallots, garlic, celery, carrot, bay leaf, and half the parsley; simmer gently for a few minutes to extract some flavour from the herbs and vegetables. Put in the mussels, cover the pan again and, shaking the pan, steam until the shells have opened (about 5 minutes); remove and discard any shells that are still closed. Lift out the mussels with a slotted spoon, leaving behind the liquor. Put them into a large bowl or tureen. Pick out the celery, carrot and bay leaf and discard. Season the liquor and, over a low heat, whisk in the butter to make a rich sauce. Sprinkle with the remaining parsley, pour the sauce over the mussels and serve immediately.

A classic dish, moules marinières is the longstanding fare of French fishermen. Sometimes the mussels are cooked in a mixture of light stock and wine or, as here, just in wine, or in a mixture of wine and water; and cream may replace, or be added to, the butter. Garlic may be omitted; different herbs may be added; and the mussels can be removed entirely from their shells or served on half shells. I add the classic court bouillon ingredients of celery, carrot and bay leaf for a well-flavoured liquor although these are usually omitted. However you cook and serve them, these steamed mussels make a superb light lunch for four people.

FRESH TROUT

ELIZA ACTON'S STEWED TROUT

*M*elt three ounces of butter in a broad stewpan, or well tinned iron saucepan, stir to it a tablespoon of flour, some mace, cayenne, and nutmeg: lay in the fish after it has been emptied, washed very clean, and wiped perfectly dry; shake it in the pan, that it may not stick, and when lightly browned on both sides, pour in three quarters of a pint of good veal stock, add a small faggot of parsley, one bay leaf, a roll of lemon-peel, and a little salt: stew the fish very gently from half to three quarters of an hour, or more, should it be unusually fine. Dish the trout, skim the fat from the gravy, and pass it through a hot strainer over the fish, which should be served immediately. A little acid can be added to the sauce at pleasure, and a glass of wine when it is considered an improvement. The receipt is for one large or for two middling-sized fish. We can recommend it as a good one from our own experience.

Butter, 3 oz.;
flour, 1 tablespoonful; seasoning of mace, cayenne, and nutmeg;
trout, 1 large, or 2 moderate-sized;
veal stock, $\frac{3}{4}$ pint; parsley, small faggot;
1 bay-leaf;
roll of lemon-rind; little salt: $\frac{1}{2}$ to $\frac{3}{4}$ hour.

A BOY'S SONG

Where the pools are
bright and deep
Where the gray trout
lies asleep,
Up the river and o'er the lea
That's the way for Billy
and me.

JAMES HOGG

A whole fresh trout stewed in spiced butter and stock, to which white wine may be added for a touch of astringency.

Cook's Tip

Nothing can be worse than over-cooked fish so remember to check its flesh. It is cooked if, when lifted with the point of a knife, it flakes cleanly away from the backbone.

MAY

When fishes leap in silver stream...
And forest bees are humming near,
And cowslips in boys' hats appear...
We then may say that May is come.

JOHN CLARE

A NUTTY CLASSIC DISH

Care must be taken when cooking the classsic French dish of trout with almonds; the nuts must be allowed to acquire a golden colour without burning, which accentuates their inherent bitterness.

THE TROUT This fish, though esteemed by the moderns for its delicacy, was little regarded by the ancients. Although it abounded in the lakes of the Roman empire, it is generally mentioned by writers only on account of the beauty of its colours. About the end of September, they quit the deep water to which they had retired during the hot weather, for the purpose of spawning. This they always do on a gravelly bottom, or where gravel and sand are mixed among stones, towards the end or by the sides of streams. At this period they become black about the head and body, and become soft and unwholesome. They are never good when they are large with roe; but there are in all trout rivers some barren female fish, which continue good throughout the winter. In the common trout, the stomach is uncommonly strong and muscular, shell-fish forming a portion of the food of the animal; and it takes into its stomach gravel or small stones in order to assist in comminuting it.

ISABELLA BEETON, *Book of Household Management (1861)*

148

TRUITES AUX AMANDES

Trout may be cooked in a huge variety of ways; really fresh fish may be simply grilled, fried, or poached. Trout may also be dipped in vinegar before they are cooked, which turns the skin blue; they can be cooked in the classic miller's fashion - à la meunière - or with wine, mushrooms and cream, or they may be baked with a stuffing or in paper parcels. However, of the many different traditional preparations of trout, this one, which is based on an old French recipe is perhaps the best known. For the fresh herbs, I like a mixture of parsley, thyme, chervil and chives but you can use just one or two types. Serves two people.

☞ *2 medium-large trout or 4 small ones, gutted*
salt and freshly milled black pepper
bunch of fresh herbs, finely chopped
plain flour, seasoned with salt, freshly milled black pepper and a pinch of cayenne
25 g/1 oz melted butter
2 tbs olive oil
40 g/1½ oz blanched flaked almonds
1 lemon, halved

Cook's Tip

The trout and almonds may be cooked entirely in the frying pan but take care not to burn the almonds; fry gently for 6–7 minutes on each side.

Have ready a shallow ovenproof dish large enough to accommodate the trout. Preheat the oven to 180°C/350°F/gas mark 4.

Wash the trout very thoroughly and drain them well. Season their cavities with salt and pepper, and push in the herbs. Dip the trout in the well-seasoned flour while you heat half the butter and half the oil in a large frying pan. When very hot put in the trout and fry briefly on both sides, just long enough to turn them golden. Put the trout into the ovenproof dish, dot with the remaining butter and put in to bake for about 15 minutes.

A few minutes before the trout are due to be ready, wipe the frying pan clean, heat the rest of the olive oil and fry the almonds until just golden brown, then add the juice of half the lemon (cut the other lemon half in two to garnish the trout). Season the trout with salt and black pepper and tip the almonds and the pan juices over them. Eat at once with boiled or steamed new potatoes and a cooked vegetable.

THE KING OF FISH

POACHED SALMON

For this dish choose firm salmon or salmon-trout fillets, which are delicious accompanied by the caper sauce (opposite) and boiled or steamed new potatoes. Thick salmon steaks can be substituted for fillets. This is enough for four people.

☞ 900 ml/ 1½ pints water
560 ml/ 1 pint dry white wine or cider
1 onion, peeled and quartered
1 carrot, scrubbed and chopped
1 celery stick, chopped
3 sprigs of fresh parsley
bay leaf
salt and freshly milled black pepper
4 salmon or salmon-trout fillets

In a covered pan bring to a boil the water, wine or cider, vegetables and herbs; season well. Cover and simmer for about 15 minutes to extract flavour. Put in the fish and poach until cooked through (8–12 minutes). Remove carefully, drain and keep warm.

CAPER SAUCE

I have adapted this from one of Eliza Acton's 'receipts', replacing some of the butter with olive oil and adding some fresh parsley for flavour. This may also be served with other fish dishes, and makes an excellent accompaniment to fried chicken.

☞ 4 tbs salted capers or capers in vinegar, washed and drained
50 g/ 2 oz butter
3 tbs olive oil
1 tbs white wine vinegar
6 sprigs parsley, finely chopped
pinch of cayenne (optional)
extra chopped parsley, to garnish

Chop the capers. Melt the butter in a small saucepan, adding the oil, chopped capers, vinegar, parsley, and cayenne (if desired). Stirring constantly, bring the sauce to simmering point, then transfer immediately into a sauceboat and pour the same over the fish while still hot, and garnish with chopped parsley.

'It wasn't the wine,' murmured Mr Snodgrass, in a broken voice, ' It was the salmon.'

CHARLES DICKENS, *Pickwick Papers*

Succulent
poached fillets of salmon
accompanied by an unusually
sharp caper sauce.

Part Seven

POULTRY & FEATHERED GAME

❦

Roasting fowl alone merits many pages, but I have chosen just two recipes, one broadly conventional, with all its trimmings, the other, a French recipe, with a coating of breadcrumbs. Tender baby chickens or poussins are best grilled, as indeed are little quails, which even in Victorian times had become scarce in some places, but farming ensures a plentiful supply these days.

This is also an opportunity to give my authentically spicy Indian recipes for poultry which, when viewed alongside the original, blander Victorian recipes relying just on curry powder that inspired them, really stimulate a good appetite.

Game birds such as partridges and pheasants, which I suspect were rather more popular then than they are today, were usually roasted, and the cooked remains were turned into wonderfully flavoured hashes and salmis. Pies were another popular destination for these hapless creatures. If, incidentally, you do not like the traditionally esteemed gamey flavour of slightly high wild fowl such as pheasants, you can of course choose very fresh, recently shot birds or even replace them with farmed guinea fowl or even a very good free-range chicken.

A plump, crisp bird roasted to perfection with a mushroom stuffing, and served with a rich gravy, herby bread sauce, and roast potatoes and parsnips.

This method of roasting always produces excellent results: a crisp, golden brown bird with succulent, perfectly cooked meat. The mushroom stuffing, the 'forcemeat' favoured by Eliza Acton, takes on a marvellous flavour and helps to keep the fowl moist, while for flavouring the bread sauce, I prefer plenty of mixed fresh herbs to the more usual cloves. Serve the bird with the stuffing, bread sauce, gravy, vegetables, roast potatoes and wonderful roast parsnips, when in season. A little currant jelly makes an excellent sweet relish to accompany the chicken.

ROAST CHICKEN WITH MUSHROOM STUFFING AND BREAD SAUCE

☞ *1 oven-ready free-range or corn-fed chicken*
freshly milled black pepper
4 tbs olive oil
4 tbs white wine
salt

Preheat the oven to 190°C/375°F/gas mark 5. Cook the stuffing and cool, then put the chicken into a suitable oven pan and stuff the chicken cavity. Sprinkle the chicken with black pepper and pour over the olive oil and wine. Roast for $1^{1}/_{4}$–$1^{1}/_{2}$ hours, basting often and turning once halfway through the roasting time. When cooked, the juices should run clear, and the skin should be crisp and golden brown. Sprinkle with salt just before serving.

MUSHROOM STUFFING

☞ *2 tbs olive oil*
$^{1}/_{2}$ onion, peeled and chopped
2 slices bacon, rinded and finely chopped
110 g/4 oz button or closed cap mushrooms, quartered
handful of fresh parsley, chopped
2 bay leaves
salt and freshly milled black pepper

Heat the oil and sauté the onion and bacon until golden, add the mushrooms and cook until coloured. Add the herbs, season and mix well. Leave to cool slightly.

BREAD SAUCE

☞ *$^{1}/_{2}$ onion, peeled and chopped*
25 g/1 oz butter
75 g/3 oz home-made breadcrumbs
225 ml/8 fl oz milk
3 tbs cream
salt and freshly milled black pepper
generous fistful of finely chopped fresh mixed herbs
(chervil, rosemary, thyme, sage, parsley, tarragon etc.)

Soften the onion in the butter. Add the breadcrumbs, milk and cream, season, and mix in the herbs. Bring to a simmer and, stirring constantly, cook until thick – a few minutes, no longer. (The bread sauce may be made in advance and reheated with a little extra milk just before the bird is carved.)

GRAVY

Pour the contents of the roasting pan into a small saucepan. Add a little olive oil or a nut of butter and 3 tbs dry sherry or brandy. Bring to the boil and stir until slightly reduced; this should only take a few minutes. Pour into a gravy boat.

'FRENCH RECEIPT' FOR CUTLETS

CHICKEN CUTLETS WITH SAUCE ESPAGNOLE

*Adapted from a 'French receipt' published in
the 1855 edition of Eliza Acton's Modern
Cookery. Serves two people, accompanied by a
green salad or lightly boiled green beans.*

☞ *2 corn-fed or free-range chicken breasts*
olive oil or butter, for frying
some good bread, sliced into 2 medium-thick pieces
(about the same size as the chicken breasts)
6 tbs fresh home-made breadcrumbs, to coat
salt and freshly milled black pepper
⅛ tsp cayenne (optional)
⅛ tsp ground mace (optional)
2 egg yolks, lightly beaten

To garnish:
chopped fresh parsley or chives
2 lemon quarters
a little Sauce Espagnole (see page 159), to serve

Skin the breast fillets. Heat 4 tbs oil or a good knob of butter in a non-stick frying pan. Fry the bread until golden brown, then remove with a slotted spoon and set aside. Wipe the pan clean (there should be very little fat left in the pan).

Mix together the breadcrumbs, seasoning, and spices (if using). Heat a small amount of fresh oil or butter in the same pan. Meanwhile dip the chicken breasts in the egg yolks, then coat with the seasoned breadcrumbs. When the oil just starts to smoke add the chicken breasts; fry both sides for about a minute, then reduce the heat and fry gently for 15–20 minutes longer, turning several times.

Put the fried bread on two plates, place the chicken breasts on top, garnish with the fresh herbs and lemon quarters, and serve a little very hot Sauce Espagnole, 'round, but not over them'.

Golden breaded chicken cutlets served up on fried bread, surrounded by a dark pool of rich Sauce Espagnole (see overleaf).

Sauce Espagnole, 'a highly-flavoured gravy' that need not be as complicated and time-consuming to prepare as some Victorian cookery books suggest. Excellent served with a wide range of meat, poultry and game dishes.

SAUCE ESPAGNOLE

*Here is a relatively quick and easy version
of a favourite Victorian sauce that varies greatly in complexity.*

☞ *25 g/ 1 oz butter*
½ carrot, scrubbed and finely diced
½ small onion, peeled and finely chopped
½ celery stick, finely chopped
1 bay leaf
2 sprigs parsley
1 sprig thyme
a very small strip of lemon peel
2 tsp flour
225 ml/ 8 fl oz beef stock
1 tsp tomato purée
1 tsp Worcestershire sauce
4 button mushrooms, very finely chopped
2 tbs dry sherry
salt and freshly milled black pepper

Heat the butter in a small non-stick frying pan and, when foaming, add the vegetables, herbs and lemon peel; fry until golden brown, but do not burn. Off the heat, stir in the flour, then return to the heat and stir around until well browned. Add the stock, tomato purée, Worcestershire sauce, mushrooms and sherry. Season and bring to the boil. Partially cover the pan, reduce the heat to minimum and simmer for 25 minutes, stirring occasionally, until the volume of liquid has reduced by half and the sauce is very dark. Strain, reheat briefly and serve as hot as possible.

A HIGHLY-FLAVOURED GRAVY

Dissolve a couple of ounces of good butter in a thick stewpan or saucepan, throw in from four to six sliced eschalots, four ounces of the lean of an undressed ham, three ounces of carrot, cut in small dice, one bay leaf, two or three branches of parsley, and one or two of thyme, but these last must be small; three cloves, a blade of mace, and a dozen corns of pepper; add part of a root of parsley, if it be at hand, and keep the whole stirred or shaken over a moderate fire for twenty minutes, then add by degrees one pint of very strong veal stock or gravy, and stew the whole gently from thirty to forty minutes; strain it, skim off the fat, and it will be ready to serve.

Butter, 2 oz.; eschalots, 4 to 6; lean of undressed ham, 4 oz.; carrots, 3 oz.; bay leaf, 1; little thyme and parsley, in branches; cloves, 3; mace, 1 blade; peppercorns, 12; little parsley root: fried gently, 20 minutes. Strong veal stock, or gravy, 1 pint: stewed very softly, 30 to 40 minutes.

ELIZA ACTON, *Modern Cookery for Private Families (1855)*

A FINE INDIAN DELICACY

FRIED MARINATED CHICKEN FILLETS

Victorian recipes absorbed little of the complexity and variety of Indian spicing, and most Victorian curries rely wholly upon curry powder, paying scant attention to the wonderful combinations of individual spices and other aromatic ingredients that Indian cooks deployed. In so far as my recipe is much closer to the spirit of Indian cooking than the one Eliza Acton borrowed (see page 163), this can hardly pass for an authentic Victorian recipe! However, it is truly delicious and vaguely mirrors her Malabar recipe, but with more authentically Indian ingredients. Serve with rice or chappati bread, a chutney, and a spicy vegetable relish.

☞ *4 tbs peanut or sunflower oil*

3 shallots, peeled and thinly sliced

3 chicken breasts, halved

1 tsp cumin seeds

1 tsp coriander seeds

1 tsp fennel seeds

small stick of cinnamon

4 cloves

¼ tsp cardamom pods (optional)

1 dried bay leaf, crumbled

¼ tsp ground turmeric

½ tsp cayenne, or to taste

4 tbs single cream or yoghurt

juice of ½ lemon or 1 lime

2 garlic cloves, peeled and crushed

salt and freshly milled black pepper

small handful of fresh chives, chopped

Heat 1 tbs of the oil in a small pan. Stir-fry the shallots until brown but not burnt. Drain on kitchen paper and reserve. Skin the chicken breasts, prick them repeatedly with the point of a sharp knife and put into a bowl. Heat the whole spices and the bay leaf in a small, heavy pan until they start to pop and smoke slightly. Shake the pan around so that they roast evenly, then tip the spices into a bowl before they burn. Grind them in a coffee grinder or pound to an aromatic powder with a pestle and mortar.

Mix together 1 tbs of the oil with all the remaining ingredients, including the ground roasted spices, but excluding the chives. Pour this marinade over the chicken breasts and turn a few times to coat them thoroughly. Cover the bowl and marinate the chicken for at least 2 hours; 6 hours is ideal.

Heat the remaining oil in a non-stick frying pan. Remove the chicken breasts from the marinade, and reserve the marinade. Discard the garlic, scrape as much marinade as possible off the chicken breasts and fry on both sides over a high heat for about 1 minute. Reduce the heat to low and cook very gently for about 15 minutes, turning once or twice. Pour off any excess fat, then add the marinade to the pan, raise the heat, and stir to dislodge the delicious pan sediments. Splash in a little water and heat through. Serve at once with the fresh chives and fried shallots sprinkled on top.

The spicy marinade improves the flavour of the chicken and the longer the marinating time, the better.

*Intensely flavoured by a highly spiced marinade, these fried
chicken breast fillets are garnished with delicious fried shallots
and fresh chives, for colour.*

CURRIED FOWL OR CHICKEN
(COLD MEAT COOKERY)

INGREDIENTS – *The remains of cold roast fowls, 2 large onions, 1 apple, 2oz. of butter, 1 dessert
spoonful of curry-powder, 1 teaspoonful of flour, ½ pint of gravy, 1 tablespoonful of lemon-juice.*
MODE – Slice the onions, peel, core, and chop the apple, and cut the fowl into neat
joints; fry these in the butter of a nice brown; then add the curry-powder, flour, and
gravy, and stew for about 20 minutes. Put in the lemon-juice, and serve with boiled rice,
either placed in a ridge round the dish or separately. Two or three shalots or a
little garlic may be added, if approved.

ISABELLA BEETON, *Book of Household Management (1861)*

SPICY FRIED CHICKEN

Eliza Acton's 'Malabar Fried Chicken', a dry dish that relies upon the best quality curry powder for rubbing into the chicken pieces, and a savoury sprinkling of onion bits fried 'as dry as chips, without the least grease or moisture upon them' to garnish.

MALABAR FRIED CHICKEN

This is an Indian dish. Cut up the chicken, wipe it dry, and rub it well with currie-powder mixed with a little salt; fry it in a bit of butter, taking care that it is of a nice light brown. In the meantime cut two or three onions into thin slices, draw them out into rings, and cut the rings into little bits about half an inch long; fry them for a long time gently in a little clarified butter, until they have gradually dried up and are of a delicate yellow-brown. Be careful that they are not burnt, as the burnt taste of a single bit would spoil the flavour of the whole. When they are as dry as chips, without the least grease or moisture upon them, mix a little salt with them, strew them over the fried chicken, and serve up with lemon on a plate.

We have extracted this receipt from a clever little work called the 'Hand-Book of Cookery.'

ELIZA ACTON, *Modern Cookery for Private Families (1855)*

MRS BEETON'S INDIAN CURRY POWDER
(FOUNDED ON DR. KITCHENER'S RECIPE)

<u>INGREDIENTS</u> – $\frac{1}{4}$ lb of coriander-seed, $\frac{1}{4}$ lb turmeric, 2 oz. cinnamon-seed, $\frac{1}{2}$ oz. of cayenne, 1 oz. of mustard, 1 oz. of ground ginger, $\frac{1}{2}$ oz. of allspice, 2 oz. of fenugreek-seed.

<u>MODE</u> – Put all the ingredients in a cool oven, where they should remain one night; then pound them in a mortar, rub them through a sieve, and mix thoroughly together; keep the powder in a bottle, from which the air should be completely excluded.

NOTE. We have given this recipe for curry-powder, as some persons prefer to make it at home; but that purchased at any respectable shop is, generally speaking, far superior, and, taking all things into consideration, very frequently more economical.

A FINE ROAST FOWL

A FRENCH RECEIPT

Fill the breast of a fine fowl with good forcemeat, roast it as usual, and when it is very nearly ready to serve take it from the fire, pour lukewarm butter over it in every part, and strew it thickly with very fine bread-crumbs; sprinkle these again with butter, and dip the fowl into more crumbs. Put it down to the fire, and when it is of a clear, light brown all over, take it carefully from the spit, dish, and serve it with lemon-sauce, and with gravy thickened and mixed with plenty of minced parsley, or with brown gravy and any other sauce usually served with fowls. Savoury herbs shred small, spice, and lemon-grate, may be mixed with the crumbs at pleasure. Do not pour gravy over the fowl when it is thus prepared.

ELIZA ACTON, *Modern Cookery for Private Families (1855)*

Cook's Tip

This tasty recipe works very well, although olive oil may readily be substituted for the butter. For the forcemeat you could use your own favourite stuffing for chicken or turkey. To make breadcrumbs: remove the crust from some stale white bread (or bake sliced fresh bread in a cool oven until slightly hard, without colouring it), tear into chunks, put them in a food processor and blend until reduced to crumbs. Breadcrumbs store well in a clean, dry airtight jar.

Eliza Acton's 'French receipt' for roasting a fowl: first the bird is roasted normally until almost ready, then rubbed all over with soft butter, to which are pressed a covering of fine breadcrumbs. Lemon sauce and gravy are the suggested accompaniments.

A FEAST TO FOLLOW THE SHOOT

*A fine game salmi or hash, a popular Victorian dish that may be prepared in variety of
ways, but always in a rich sauce made with a stock from the birds' carcasses.*

SALMI DE PERDREAUX; SALMI OF PARTRIDGES

Par-roast three or four partridges kept till they have taken a little fumet. When cold, skin
and carve them. Put them into a small stew-pan, with a bit of lemon-peel, four eschalots,
a few bits of dressed ham, seasoning herbs of all kinds that you like, and a dessert-spoonful of
peppercorns, with the trimmings of the partridges, a half-pint of Espagnole, and two glasses of
Madeira. Let this simmer for an hour very gently. Dish the birds, and strain the skimmed sauce
hot over them. Serve fried bread with the salmi, which must be very hot and high-seasoned to be
good for any thing.

MEG DODS, *Cook and Housewife's Manual (1829)*

SALMI OF FOWL

Salmi or hash of game birds was a very popular Victorian dish, especially with shooting parties, following a successful shoot. This rich recipe works equally well with mixed or just one species of fowl, and serves four people, accompanied by potatoes and vegetables.

☞ *1 young pheasant and 2 partridges, or a brace of young pheasants, oven-ready*
110 g / 4 oz butter, or butter and olive oil
4–6 slices streaky bacon
75 g / 3 oz ham, diced small
200 g / 7 oz closed cup or button mushrooms, halved if large
6–8 shallots, peeled and chopped
1 celery stick, thinly sliced
1 carrot, scrubbed and finely chopped
3 cloves
¼ tsp ground mace
⅛ tsp cayenne
2 bay leaves
2–3 sprigs thyme
2–3 sprigs parsley
salt and freshly milled black pepper
juice of ½ lemon
560 ml / 1 pint beef stock
225 ml / 8 fl oz dry sherry
3–4 slices white bread, quartered and fried golden brown in oil

Preheat the oven to 200°C/400°F/gas mark 6. Rub the birds with a little butter or olive oil and put a knob of butter inside each one. Wrap their breasts with bacon. Roast for about 20 minutes, basting several times. Cool, then remove all the skin. Cut up the birds' breasts and legs. Put flesh into a shallow pan or casserole and set aside.

Put the skin and carcasses into a large pan together with a covering of water – no more than 560 ml/1 pint. Bring to the boil, then simmer, tightly covered, for an hour.

Heat the remaining butter or butter and oil and briefly fry the ham. Add the mushrooms, shallots, vegetables, spices and herbs and stir-fry for about 5 minutes longer or until pale golden. Season, then pour in the lemon juice, the game stock and the beef stock, then reduce over a high heat for about 12 minutes or until the volume of liquid is reduced by half. Add the sherry and simmer, uncovered, for 5 minutes longer. Saving the mushrooms, strain the sauce into the casserole containing the fowl. Cover the casserole and simmer for about 10 minutes together with the mushrooms. Check the seasoning and serve at once over the fried bread.

'AN EXCELLENT LUNCHEON'

CHICKEN À LA MAYONNAISE

The Victorians had a taste for cold meats and fowl dressed with mayonnaise. Isabella Beeton recommended that 'all kinds of cold meat and solid fish may be dressed à la mayonnaise, and make excellent luncheon or supper dishes'. For the best flavour do make your own mayonnaise, and try to buy free-range or corn-fed chickens. This serves four people.

☞ *1 free-range or corn-fed chicken, roasted and cooled*
6 tbs mayonnaise
2 tbs water
pinch of cayenne
1 lettuce heart ('little gem' lettuces are perfect)
bunch of watercress, stems trimmed
3 hard-boiled eggs, peeled and sliced into rings

Carve the chicken neatly, removing the skin, and arrange the meat on a large serving dish. Thin the mayonnaise with the water and dress the chicken meat with it. Dust lightly with cayenne. Wash and thoroughly shake dry the lettuce hearts and watercress. Separate the lettuce leaves and surround the chicken with the salad leaves and the egg rings.

Cook's Tip

Should the mayonnaise fail to emulsify add another egg yolk, a little more mustard and a very thin trickle of oil and beat again until thick.

MAYONNAISE

Although the Victorians were obliged to beat or whisk emulsified sauces, the food processor is a quick and reliable tool for mayonnaise-making. To emulsify properly the eggs must be at room temperature. The oil has to be added very slowly, almost drop by drop. A mixture of olive and sunflower oils produces a lighter mayonnaise than the traditional version made entirely with olive oil, which has a rather intrusive flavour. For this reason, extra virgin olive oil is unsuitable. This makes about 225 ml/ 8 fl oz.

☞ *2 egg yolks, at room temperature*
1/2 tsp salt
2 tsp wine vinegar or lemon juice
1 tsp mustard
200 ml/ 7 fl oz oil

Put the egg yolks, salt, vinegar or lemon juice and mustard into the bowl of a food processor. With the motor running, add the oil in a very thin, steady stream; stop the motor as soon as all the oil has been used up and the mayonnaise is thick and glossy.

You could, of course, cheat and use a good commercial brand of mayonnaise, but don't thin it.

Delicious cold chicken dressed with flavourful home-made mayonnaise: a simple but satisfying Victorian treat.

FEATHERED GAME PIE

Pheasant, partridge or guinea fowl are all delicious turned into a rich pie whose flavour is enhanced by bacon, aromatic vegetables and herbs, mushrooms, and a good winey stock; ready-made pastry is a labour-saving God-send for making the pie lid.

Cook's Tip

Although the game stock gives a superior flavour, 225 ml/8 fl oz chicken stock made with a stock cube may be substituted. If so, omit the whole parsley stalks, celery, carrot and one onion.

PHEASANT PIE

Use any feathered game for this pie; pheasant is suitable but you could also include other fowl such as partridge, guinea fowl, and even well-flavoured free-range or corn-fed chicken or turkey breast-meat. I like to add equal measures of white wine and game stock which, when reduced to a thick sauce give an exceptionally good flavour. Serves four, accompanied by vegetables or a salad.

☞ *1 oven-ready pheasant and 2 guinea fowl or chicken breasts*
handful of fresh parsley, including some whole sprigs with stalks
2 celery sticks, chopped
1 carrot, scrubbed and chopped
2 large onions, peeled and chopped
salt and freshly milled black pepper
4 tbs olive oil or 50 g/2 oz butter
110 g/4 oz lean bacon, rinded and cut into small strips
225 g/8 oz mushrooms, halved or quartered
225 ml/8 fl oz dry white wine
2 bay leaves
2 sprigs thyme
350 g/12 oz puff or shortcrust pastry, thawed if frozen

Remove the pheasant breasts and the leg meat (if liked) and cut into 4 cm/1½ inch chunks. Cube the guinea fowl or chicken breasts. Chop half the parsley. Put the pheasant carcass into a stewing pan together with the whole sprigs of parsley, the celery, carrot, 1 onion, and about 1 litre/1¾ pints of water. Season and bring to the boil, then cover the pan, reduce the heat and simmer for at least 1 hour. Strain the stock and measure out about 225 ml/8 fl oz; (keep or freeze the rest).

Heat the oil or butter in another pan and fry the bacon and the remaining onion until they begin to colour. Add the fowl and fry until golden. (If using guinea fowl or chicken meat remove now as it cooks more quickly than pheasant.) Add the mushrooms and stir-fry for about 5 minutes. Pour in the wine and stock, and add the bay leaves, thyme and remaining parsley. Cook down to a fairly dense but not dry stew, returning the chicken for the last 15 minutes or so of cooking; this should take about 35 minutes in total, and you may have to raise the heat to reduce the liquid. Season, allow to cool slightly, and remove the bay leaves. Empty the pan contents into a pie dish.

Preheat the oven to 200°C/400°F/gas mark 6. Roll out the pastry to overlap the rim of the dish with some margin. Cut a long thin pastry strip to fit around the rim of the pie dish. Moisten the rim and stick the pastry strip to it. Moisten the top surface of the pastry rim and fit the pastry lid to it. Press together to seal, if necessary moistening with a little more water. (Unless the lid is secure the pastry may shrink and the pie dry out.) Decorate with any scraps of pastry, pierce the lid and bake for about 25 minutes or until golden brown.

This pie is also delicious eaten cold; serve with salad or coleslaw.

SPATCHCOCKED POUSSINS

POUSSINS WITH MUSTARD

Poussins (baby chickens) are delicious when simply seasoned, wiped with butter, and grilled. However a creamy mustard marinade such as this one does not overwhelm their sweet, delicate flavour, and it cooks to a crisp dark crust keeping the flesh within deliciously moist and succulent. To spatchcock a poussin, first cut along each side of the backbone with poultry shears or scissors, and remove the bone. Open out the bird so that the breasts and legs are splayed and skin-side up. Trim off any ragged skin. Always choose small, young birds. This recipe serves two people.

☞ *2 poussins*
1 heaped tbs wholegrain mustard
3 tbs single cream
1 tbs white wine vinegar
salt and freshly milled black pepper
leaves from 2–3 sprigs fresh tarragon, chopped

Spatchcock the poussins as already described above. In a bowl, mix together the mustard, cream, vinegar, seasoning and tarragon. Prick the poussins' skin repeatedly with a fork to allow the mustard sauce to penetrate, and spread with the dressing. Cover the poussins and leave to marinate for several hours – the longer the better.

Preheat the grill, then scorch the poussins for 12–15 minutes or until well browned. Baste once or twice with any remaining marinade. If the poussins threaten to burn before they are thoroughly cooked, move them to a lower position farther from the heat source. Serve with steamed or boiled new potatoes, tossed in butter and fresh parsley or chives, and seasoned with a generous grinding of black pepper. Alternatively, serve with mashed potatoes and celeriac.

Grilled, spatchcocked baby chickens need the added flavour imparted by a creamy mustard marinade. This flavours the sweet flesh but also chars agreeably, preserving the birds' moisture within.

AN EASTERN PREPARATION

With its essential flavourings of anchovy (or a derivative such as Worcestershire sauce), and chilli vinegar, burdwan is an excellent savoury use for leftover cooked chicken.

Burdwan features as an entreé in many Victorian cookery books and recipe collections. Eliza Acton, from whom this recipe is adapted, called it 'an Oriental dish of high savour, which may be made either with a young fowl or chicken parboiled for the purpose, or with the remains of such as have already been sent to the table'. Most other recipes share the latter, utilitarian option, making this a classic Victorian leftover dish. I would add that, to anyone with access to a halfway decent Indian restaurant, this dish will seem far from authentic, but was chosen instead as an example of how the Victorians adapted Indian food to suit their tastes and available ingredients. Serves four people, accompanied by pilau rice and an Indian chutney or relish.

INDIAN BURDWAN

☞ *50 g / 2 oz butter*
4–6 shallots, peeled and very finely chopped
1 garlic clove, peeled and chopped
½ tsp flour
¼ tsp cayenne
170 ml / 6 fl oz water
110 ml / 4 fl oz sherry or Madeira
1 tbs Worcestershire sauce
1 tbs chilli vinegar or 1 tbs wine vinegar and 1 fresh green chilli, seeded and finely chopped
450 g / 1 lb cooked boneless chicken, in pieces
small handful of fresh parsley, chopped

Heat the butter in a frying pan. When just frothing add the shallots and garlic and stir-fry until lightly coloured. Stir in the flour and cayenne, fry for a minute, then pour in the water, sherry, Worcestershire sauce, and chilli vinegar. Bring to the boil, stirring, then reduce the heat and simmer gently for about 10 minutes or until thick. Put in the chicken, mix well with the sauce, cover the pan, then raise the heat to medium-low and cook for about 5 minutes longer. Sprinkle lightly with parsley and serve immediately.

Olive oil or peanut oil may be substituted for the butter.

POULTRY OF ALL KINDS, DEVILLED – These are best made by poultry previously cooked. Place in the pan one ounce only of butter, and fry gently until hot through. A slight improvement may be made in using the frying-pan; it is to rub the bottom with garlic or eschalot before placing the fat in, frying some onions the same time.

ALEXIS SOYER, *A Shilling Cookery for the People (1859)*

MEG DODS' INDIAN BURDWAN

This eastern preparation is of the English genus, devil, or French Salmi. It is made of cold poultry, rabbits, venison, kid, game, but is best of the latter. Make a sauce of melted butter with cayenne, or a fresh Chili if possible; a bit of garlic, essence of anchovy, and a sliced Spanish onion. Stew until the onion is pulpy, when the Burdwan will be ready. Squeeze in a lime or Seville orange. Serve round very hot.

It would be very easy to swell this section of the MANUAL with a formidable array of uncouth dishes and strange names, with Indian, Syrian, Turkish, and Persian Yaughs, kabaubs, and Cuscussuies, &c. as modern travellers, and particularly the French, have paid considerable attention to Asiatic cookery; but this we consider mere waste of space, which may be more usefully employed.

MEG DODS *Cook and Housewife's Manual (1829)*

SMALL GRILLED FOWL

QUAILS À LA POLONAISE

This is the name given in France to small fowl when grilled with a coating of minced parsley mixed together with finely chopped eggs and fine breadcrumbs. Even in Victorian Britain wild quails had become scarce; as Mrs Beeton observed, 'they are not very numerous'. However, good quality farmed quails are available all year round, but other small game birds or even very small poussins may be substituted. This recipe serves two people, with a watercress garnish.

☞ *4 free-range oven-ready quails or 2 poussins*
salt and freshly milled black pepper
50 g/2 oz butter, melted
1 hardboiled egg
25 g/1 oz fine breadcrumbs
handful of fresh parsley, finely chopped
1 lemon, quartered
sprigs of watercress

Preheat the grill. Spatchcock the quails (see Spatchcocked Poussins, page 172), and place them side by side in a shallow heatproof pan or tray that will fit under the grill. Season them all over and brush them with a little of the melted butter. Chop the hardboiled egg as finely as possible, and mix in a bowl with the breadcrumbs and parsley.

When the grill is very hot, put in the quails. Grill one side until golden, turn and grill the others side, then remove and brush again with a little melted butter, saving enough for a final coating. Spread the egg and breadcrumb mixture liberally over the quails. Sprinkle with the remaining melted butter on top and return to the grill, the breasts facing up. Remove when the coating is crisp and brown but not burnt. Garnish with the lemon quarters and sprigs of watercress, and serve straight away.

TO DRESS QUAILS

INGREDIENTS – Quails, butter, toast
MODE – These birds keep good several days, and should be roasted without drawing. Truss them in the same manner as woodcocks; roast them before a clear fire, keep them well basted, and serve on toast.
TIME – About 20 minutes

ISABELLA BEETON,
Book of Household Management (1861)

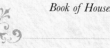

Little quails à la Polonaise, spatchcocked and grilled until golden coated with fine breadcrumbs mixed with parsley and finely chopped egg.

The popular Victorian game hash (in this case quails); fried bread is the perfect base for leftover fowl heated through in a rich, spicy, dark sauce.

QUAIL HASH

This Victorian recipe provides a convenient way to use up any leftover roasted game birds; to test the recipe I used the cooked flesh of five quails, and the hash was sufficient for two people.

☞ 25 g/ 1 oz butter
2 shallots, peeled and chopped
1 bay leaf
2 sprigs thyme
$\frac{1}{8}$ tsp ground mace
$\frac{1}{8}$–$\frac{1}{4}$ tsp cayenne
salt and freshly milled black pepper
1 tsp flour
560 ml/ 1 pint chicken stock (or stock made with the fowls' skin and carcasses)
225 ml/ 8 fl oz full-bodied red wine
6 tbs port or Madeira
225 g/ 8 oz cooked, skinned game flesh
juice of $\frac{1}{2}$ lemon
4 triangles fried bread

*H*eat the butter; when foaming add the shallots and the herbs to the pan and sauté until soft. Stir in the spices, season, and add the flour. Pour in the stock, wine, and port or Madeira, and bring to the boil. Boil down to a thick sauce; the reduction of liquid should be at least two-thirds of the original volume. Add the game, sprinkle with the lemon juice and heat through for a few minutes, without boiling. Serve next to the fried bread triangles.

*S*erenely full, the epicure would say,
Fate cannot harm me, for I have
dined today.

SYDNEY SMITH

Give me the clear blue sky above my head, and the green turf beneath my feet, a winding road before me, and a three hours' march to dinner...

WILLIAM HAZLITT

Part Eight
MEAT &
FURRED GAME

JUICY BEEF, succulent veal, strong
mutton and sweet tender lamb, abundant, flavoursome pork, dark rich venison,
gamey rabbits and the even gamier, esteemed
flesh of the mysterious hare – meat from every
kind of animal was right at the very core of
the Victorian kitchen and was rarely, if ever,
absent from affluent dining tables.

One imagines that for those Victorians
able to afford it, eating meat was a much more
enjoyable experience than it has become
today. Fortunately, some shops are now sell-
ing traditionally matured, organic beef, and
fresh, seasonal lamb has never really suffered
from a decline in quality. And if you are fortunate to have enjoyed the services of a good
butcher you may find all this gloomy talk
unfamiliar and alarmist!

Roasting was undoubtedly the preferred
cooking method, but boiling was also popular,
although I dislike the plainer boiled meats for
which recipes abound in Victorian cookery
books. Grilling with a gridiron was another
common technique, and frying was and remains
very good for certain cuts. Yet perhaps best of
all are the delicious slowly cooked dishes, the
rich melting stews and wonderful comforting
pies that turn meat-eating into an almost
sensual experience.

MR PICKWICK'S LAMB CHOPS

Lamb chops served up with creamy mashed potatoes, vegetables and a well-flavoured tomato sauce enhanced with a little sherry and cayenne make a fine supper or lunch dish.

Although the Victorians loved the strong flavour of mutton, lamb is a sweeter, more readily available meat that is generally preferred today. (Mutton) 'chops and tomata sauce' was a favourite dish of Dickens's memorable character, Mr Pickwick. This recipe serves four.

GRILLED LAMB CHOPS WITH TOMATO SAUCE

If you can get good fresh lamb cutlets they will be especially sweet and tender. A cast-iron griddle with a raised ridge, preheated until very hot is perhaps the best device for 'grilling' the meat, since this method imparts a smoky flavour akin to char-grilling and the ridge leaves attractive sear marks upon the flesh.

TOMATO SAUCE

☞ *8 ripe tomatoes*
2 tbs olive oil
1 carrot, peeled and chopped
1 celery stick, chopped
3 shallots, peeled and chopped
2 cloves (optional)
salt to taste
¼ tsp cayenne
2 tbs dry sherry
110 ml/ 4 fl oz chicken or vegetable stock

LAMB CHOPS

☞ *4 thick lamb chops or 8 small lamb cutlets*
freshly milled black pepper
olive oil
salt

Bring a pan of water to the boil. When boiling steadily, plunge in the tomatoes, then remove them with a slotted spoon after 30 seconds. Allow to cool, then remove the skins, which should slip off very easily. Chop the tomatoes finely, discarding the seeds. Heat the oil in a pan. Sauté the carrots, celery and shallots until golden brown. Add the chopped tomatoes and the remaining sauce ingredients. Simmer for 30 minutes, then sieve through a wire strainer into a clean pan. Set aside.

Preheat a grill, cast-iron griddle or a large, heavy frying pan. Season the chops with black pepper, then dip them in olive oil. Grill on both sides until done to the required degree of pinkness. Sprinkle with salt when cooked. Reheat the sauce briefly and serve it hot beside the chops, accompanied by mashed or sautéed potatoes, and a vegetable.

Cook's Tip

Out of season, it is better to substitute the chopped contents of a 400 g/14 oz can of plum tomatoes. Unless the fresh tomatoes are very sweet, add a pinch of sugar. Fillet or rump steaks grilled in exactly the same way are equally well complemented by the tomato sauce.

COMFORTING WINTER STEW

RICH LAMB STEW WITH BEANS

Lamb, whether roasted or stewed, is traditionally paired with beans which render potatoes superfluous, although a cooked vegetable or a salad would not go amiss. This fine recipe makes a deliciously comforting winter dish. Like most rich stews it actually improves for being kept overnight and then reheated. This makes enough for four people.

☞ *250 g / 9 oz haricot (navy) beans*
900 g / 2 lb lean boned lamb
6 tbs olive oil (or oil and butter)
50 g / 2 oz bacon, rinded, cut into small strips
1 carrot, peeled and sliced
1 celery stick, sliced
10–12 shallots, peeled (half chopped, half left whole)
560 ml / 1 pint red wine
1 tbs tomato purée
2 tsp Worcestershire sauce
1 bay leaf, 2–3 sprigs parsley, 1 sprig marjoram, tied together
salt and freshly milled black pepper

Put the beans in a bowl and cover with water. Leave them overnight or for at least 6 hours. Preheat the oven to 190°C/375°F/ gas mark 5. Drain the beans and put them into an ovenproof casserole with a good covering of fresh salted water (about 1.1 litres/2 pints). Cover, bring to the boil, remove any scum, then transfer to the oven and bake for at least 1½ hours or until the beans are soft and almost all the water has been absorbed. Stir occasionally and add a little more water if necessary.

Meanwhile trim away all the fat and cube the lamb, ensuring that all the chunks are of roughly equal size.

In a large saucepan heat the oil and brown the lamb in batches, then remove and put on one side. Fry the bacon until coloured, then sauté the carrot, celery and shallots until lightly coloured. Return the lamb to the pan, pour in the wine and add the tomato purée, Worcestershire sauce and herbs. Season, combine thoroughly and bring to the boil. Reduce to a simmer and cook, partly covered, for about 1¾ hours, stirring occasionally and checking that the lamb does not dry out or stick to the bottom of the pan (remedy if necessary with a little water).

Divide the beans between four warmed plates, remove the herbs and serve the lamb stew over the beans.

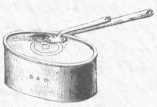

*A wonderful lamb stew cooked
with shallots, and served with its traditional
bean accompaniment; this is ideal cold-weather
fare, and the stew tastes even better
reheated the next day.*

TENDER RUMP STEAKS

*Devilled rump steaks, inspired by the great Alexis Soyer's recipe,
with a tangy flavour imparted by a marinade of olive oil, vinegar,
cayenne and mustard.*

DEVILLED RUMP STEAKS

These deliciously tangy steaks are very simple to cook and make a fine quick lunch or supper, allowing the busy cook to get on with other things while the steaks marinate. Accompany with Soyer's fried potatoes and one of the salads from this book. This serves two people.

☞ *2 x 175 g / 6 oz rump steaks*
1 tbs olive oil
1 tbs garlic vinegar, red wine vinegar or sherry vinegar
½ tsp cayenne
2 heaped tbs grain mustard
freshly milled black pepper
fine crystal sea salt

Trim off the excess fat but leave a thin rind attached to the steaks to keep them moist. Put them on a plate. Mix together the remaining ingredients except for the salt and spread over both sides of the steaks, ensuring that they are well coated. Cover with another plate and put to one side for at least 2 hours. When ready to cook, heat a heavy griddle or cast iron frying pan until very hot (or preheat the grill). Cook the steaks for just 1 or 2 minutes on each side, depending upon thickness, or until done to your liking; allow 2–3 minutes for well-done steaks. Sprinkle with salt and eat straight away.

SOYER'S 'LESSON' FOR BROILING STEAKS

First Lesson - For first quality of steak, the meat ought to be well hung, and if cut nicely off the rump of a Scotch beast will weigh from a pound and a quarter to a pound and a half, that is, being three-quarters of an inch thick; if it should be cut rather thicker in one part than another, beat it even with a chopper; if of the above thickness, it should be placed about five inches above the fire; if thicker, six inches; taking it as an invariable rule, that the thicker the steak, the further in proportion it must be from the fire. The extra piece of fat which accompanies it should be put on a little after the steak, or it will be too much done. Whilst doing, throw over some pepper and salt, and turn it the moment the fat begins to drop: the motive of constantly turning the steak is to keep the gravy in. Never put a fork into it to turn it, but use a pair of tongs but if you have not any, place the fork in the fat and turn it. When the steak is done, it will feel firm under the pressure of the finger.

ALEXIS SOYER, *A Shilling Cookery for the People (1859)*

OLD ENGLAND'S ROAST BEEF

There is no finer Sunday lunch than a good joint of beef, with light, fluffy Yorkshire pudding, crisp roast potatoes with soft mealy middles, vegetables, gravy made with the juices from the roasting pan, and a little pungent English mustard or horseradish sauce.

Roast beef has long been a national dish in England. In most of our patriotic songs it is contrasted with the fricasséed frogs, popularly supposed to be the exclusive diet of Frenchmen.

ISABELLA BEETON, *Book of Household Management (1861)*

ROAST BEEF

The Victorians generally roasted on a spit; Victorian recipes specify 'place near to the fire', and 'when the steam from the meat draws strongly towards the fire, it is nearly or quite ready to serve', and few would argue that spit-roasting over a good flame produces excellent roasts. However, we have to make do with modern ovens, which must be preheated to their highest temperature for the initial blast of heat to seal in the valuable meat juices. Allow 20 minutes for sealing, then reduce the oven temperature to 190°C/375°F/gas mark 5, and roast for 15 minutes per pound (450 g/1 lb) of meat for a rare roast, 20 minutes for medium, and 25 minutes for well done meat. Weigh the joint and calculate the cooking time in advance, but remember that this time should be added on to the initial 20 minutes for sealing the beef. Good cuts for roasting are silverside, sirloin, rib, rump and fillet. The best beef will have been hung for a few weeks both to develop flavour and to tenderize the meat. Alas, because it is less profitable, well-hung, additive-free beef has become rather scarce unless you are fortunate enough to know a good independent butcher.

☞ *joint of beef*
freshly milled black pepper
olive oil

Preheat the oven. Put the joint in a roasting tin. Season the beef all over with black pepper and rub with olive oil. Roast as directed (see left), basting a few times with the pan juices, and turning once. Sprinkle with salt towards the end of the cooking time. When cooked, transfer the joint to a warmed serving platter.

To make the gravy, heat the roasting pan on top of the stove to brown the juices and the flavourful sediment. Deglaze the pan with a wine glass of beef stock (broth) or water and an equal measure of red wine or dry sherry. Stir to dislodge the sediment, season generously with salt and pepper, and boil down to half the volume of liquid, stirring frequently. Add to the pan any further meat juices that may have collected on the serving platter, stir in a good nut of butter, mix well, and pour into a gravy boat.

Carve the beef and serve with the gravy and horseradish sauce or English mustard, gravy, Yorkshire pudding, roast potatoes – and always a favourite – roast parsnips, when in season, alongside a green vegetable.

When the potatoes are roasted, slightly squeeze each separately in a cloth, to make them mealy, then split them open; season them with a bit of butter, or dripping, a little bit of chopped shalot, pepper, and salt, and this will afford you a nice relish for supper.

CHARLES ELMÉ FRANCATELLI, *A Plain Cookery Book for the Working Classes* (1861)

HEARTY STEAK PIE

Shortcrust or flaky puff pastry can be used for this rich steak and mushroom pie; the pastry itself is sufficient in the way of a starchy accompaniment.

STEAK AND MUSHROOM PIE

Here is a fine recipe for a delicious hearty steak pie that serves four people, accompanied by a vegetable or a salad. Puff pastry, which can be bought ready-made, makes a particularly attractive pie.

☞ *900 g / 2 lb steak*
4 tbs olive oil (or olive oil and butter)
110 g / 4 oz lean bacon, rinded and chopped
8 shallots, peeled and chopped
1 carrot, scrubbed and diced
1 celery stick, diced
350 g / 12 oz button or closed cup mushrooms, halved or quartered if large
salt and freshly milled black pepper
1 tbs tomato purée (optional)
1 bay leaf
2 tsp Worcestershire sauce
225 ml / 8 fl oz beef stock
560 ml / 1 pint red wine
350 g / 12 oz shortcrust or puff pastry

Trim off all the fat and cut the steak into 4 cm / 1½ inch cubes. Heat the oil and sauté the bacon, shallots, carrot and celery until soft and lightly coloured. Add the steak and stir-fry until no longer raw-looking. Add the mushrooms and stir-fry for 4–6 minutes longer. Season well, stir in the tomato purée (if using) and add the bay leaf, Worcestershire sauce, stock and wine. Bring to the boil, then reduce the heat, cover, and simmer for 1¼ hours. Uncover and simmer for about 15 minutes longer. The stew should now be thick but quite saucy; put it into a pie dish.

Preheat the oven to 200°C/400°F/gas mark 6. Roll out the pastry to overlap the rim of the pie dish, leaving some margin. Cut a long thin pastry strip to fit around the rim of the pie dish. Moisten the rim and stick the pastry strip to it. Moisten the top surface of the pastry rim and fit the pastry lid to it. Press together to seal, if necessary moistening with a little more water. (Unless the lid is secure the pastry may shrink and the pie dry out.) Decorate with any spare scraps of pastry, pierce the lid and bake for about 25 minutes or until the crust is a beautiful, deep golden brown.

A ONE-POT MEAL

BEEF STEW WITH DUMPLINGS

This stew is made substantial by plenty of vegetables and the addition of dumplings, providing an excellent complete meal that needs no further accompaniment. The stew tastes even better when reheated the day after it is cooked but do not add the dumplings until half an hour before you are due to serve; you may also need to add a little more water to the stew to submerge the dumplings, which will keep their shape well in the stew. They are filling and very comforting! Makes enough for four people.

☞ *1 bay leaf*
3–4 sprigs parsley
3 sprigs thyme
3–4 sprigs of chervil
thin strip of lemon peel
$^1/_2$ celery stick
900 g/ 2 lb tail end of rump or good stewing steak
flour, to coat the beef
4 tbs olive oil (or oil and butter)
3 slices lean bacon, rinded and diced
1 large onion, peeled and chopped
6 pickling onions or shallots, peeled
2 large carrots, scrubbed and coarsely chopped
3 small turnips, peeled and cubed
3 cloves
$^1/_8$ tsp cayenne
1 tsp paprika
$^1/_8$ tsp ground mace
1 tbs brandy
280 ml/ $^1/_2$ pint dry white wine
560 ml/ 1 pint veal stock or water
salt and freshly milled black pepper

Tie together the herbs, lemon peel and celery. Trim the steak of all fat and cut into 3cm/ 1$^1/_4$ inch cubes. Coat lightly in flour.

Heat the oil in a large pan. Brown the beef evenly in batches and remove to a plate. Fry the bacon, chopped onion, pickling onions, carrots and turnip pieces until lightly coloured, then remove the turnips and pickling onions and reserve them. Return the beef to the pan. Push in the celery and herb bundle, add the spices and pour in the brandy, wine and stock or water. Season well and bring to the boil. Cover, reduce the heat and leave to simmer for 1 hour, stirring occasionally. Return the pickling onions and turnips to the pan, mix, cover again and continue to simmer for another hour.

Start making the dumplings about 45 minutes before the end of the cooking time.

HARD DUMPLINGS

☞ *175 g/ 6 oz plain flour, plus extra for handling*
140 ml/ 5 fl oz water
$^1/_2$ teaspoon salt

Mix the flour, water and salt to a smooth, thick, sticky batter. With floured hands form into six small, sticky dumplings. Raise the heat of the stew, add to it a little extra water and, when boiling, introduce the dumplings, ensuring that they are completely submerged. After a few minutes, reduce the heat, cover again and simmer for about 30 minutes. Remove the herb and celery bundle before serving.

A very traditional beef stew, with flour dumplings and three different vegetables all cooked in the same pot, making a complete, nourishing and filling meal.

VEAL SUPPER FOR FOUR

Veal escalopes cook very quickly, but if boredom is to be avoided the slightly bland meat needs a good rich sauce such as this one made with mushrooms, cream and sherry, the latter adding a delicious spicy note. This is similar in character to the Italian dish scaloppine alla Marsala.

VEAL ESCALOPES WITH MUSHROOMS, CREAM AND SHERRY

This is a very quick and delicious lunch or supper for four people; fried or sautéed potatoes and a cooked vegetable or salad are the ideal accompaniments. Alternatively, serve with rice.

☞ 4 thin veal escalopes (about 450 g/ 1 lb)
freshly milled black pepper
plain flour, for coating
40 g/ 1½ oz butter
salt
225 g/ 8 oz baby button mushrooms, cleaned but left whole
110 ml/ 4 fl oz dry sherry
110 ml/ 4 fl oz double cream
small handful of fresh parsley, chopped

Trim off any surplus fat from the escalopes, then place them between sheets of clear plastic and beat out with a wooden mallet or a rolling pin, but without tearing the meat. Season with pepper, dip them in flour and shake off the excess.

Heat half the butter in a large frying pan; when foaming put in 2 escalopes. Fry until golden, then turn and fry the other side until golden. Sprinkle with salt and keep warm. Repeat for the remaining escalopes. In the same pan heat the remaining butter. Stir-fry the whole mushrooms until golden, then pour in the sherry, and let the liquid thicken. Season, add the cream and parsley and return the veal; heat through, and serve immediately.

ON VEAL

Procure about 1 lb. veal, either from the leg, the chump-end of the loin, or best end of the neck: cut this into round or oval scollops, season with pepper and salt, and place them in a sautapan with some clarified butter: an equal number of similarly-cut scollops of ham may either be put with these, or separately. Fry the veal and ham scollops nicely brown, pour off the grease, add the brown Italian sauce and some button-mushrooms; simmer the whole together for three minutes, dish them up, alternately placing a scollop of veal with the ham; fill the centre with the mushrooms, pour the sauce round the entrée, and serve.

CHARLES ELMÉ FRANCATELLI,
The Modern Cook (1896)

BAKED IN BATTER

SAUSAGE TOAD IN THE HOLE

*T*his recipe merely requires good quality butcher's sausages
and may seem pedestrian by comparison to the above! However,
I have kept Soyer's original eggy batter recipe, which makes a very
light and delicious dish, serving four people.

☞ *12 large, best-quality pork sausages*
   (about 675 g/ 1½ lb)
175 g/ 6 oz plain flour
4 eggs
1 tsp salt
½ tsp pepper
560ml/ 1 pint semi-skimmed milk
¼ tsp freshly grated nutmeg (optional)

*P*reheat the oven to 220°C/425°F/gas mark 7. Grease a large ovenproof dish and put the sausages in to bake. Meanwhile mix the remaining ingredients together to form a smooth batter, and let it rest. Turn the sausages once or twice, and, when lightly browned all over, pour in the batter and bake for about 30 minutes longer or until the batter is well risen and golden.

Although sausages have since become the norm, in Victorian times toad in the hole meant any kind or cut of meat baked partly or fully submerged in a batter. Like that other great British dish, bangers and mash, this is a favourite with children and adults alike.

*This simple rabbit ragoût is very closely based on
Mrs Beeton's original recipe published in her classic*
Book of Household Management.

RAGOÛT OF RABBIT OR HARE

Ready-jointed rabbit is increasingly to be found in supermarkets, although in Victorian times it was a far more commonly available meat. By comparison, in southern Europe rabbits have never declined in popularity, and have long been sold live in markets. Mrs Beeton wrote that the flesh of the wild rabbit was 'considered to have a higher flavour than that of the tame rabbit, although it is neither so white nor so delicate.' This is based closely on her recipe, and serves four people.

☞ 50 g/2 oz butter
4 slices bacon, rinded and diced
2 large onions, peeled and chopped
1 carrot, scrubbed and diced
3 tsp flour
1 kg/2¼ lb skinned and jointed rabbit
salt and freshly milled black pepper
2 slices lemon
1 bay leaf
110 ml/4 fl oz cup port

Heat the butter in a stewing pan, add the bacon, onion and carrot and fry to a rich golden colour. Stir in the flour and gradually add enough water to give a creamy consistency to the sauce. Add the rabbit pieces, season, and put in the lemon slices and the bay leaf. Raise the heat, and when bubbling, reduce the heat, cover and simmer for 40–45 minutes, stirring a few times. Pour in the port, bring back to the boil, cook fast for a few minutes, then serve.

CATALAN RABBIT STEW

In the Catalan region of Spain, aromatic pastes of nuts, herbs, saffron and garlic called picadas have traditionally thickened rich stews. This serves four people.

☞ 4 tbs olive oil
1 kg/2¼ lb skinned and jointed rabbit
1 large onion, peeled and chopped
1 large carrot, peeled and diced
1 celery stick, thinly sliced
2 tbs tomato purée
280 ml/10 fl oz dry white wine
1 tbs brandy
salt and freshly milled black pepper
2 garlic cloves, peeled
50 g/2 oz shelled hazelnuts, blanched almonds
or pine nuts
handful of fresh parsley,
pinch of saffron threads
2 tbs extra virgin olive oil

Heat the olive oil in a large casserole. Brown and remove the rabbit pieces. Fry the onion, carrot and celery in the oil until pale golden. Return the rabbit pieces to the pan, add the tomato purée, pour in the wine and brandy, season, and bring to the boil. Reduce the heat, cover, and simmer for 35 minutes.

Meanwhile, with a pestle and mortar pound to a paste the garlic, nuts, parsley and saffron, then stir in the oil and a pinch of salt (or grind everything to a paste in a food processor). Add to the casserole and simmer for 10 minutes. Serve with potatoes and a vegetable.

RICH AND WARMING ROAST

STRACOTTO

My version of this classic pot-roast from the north of Italy is rich and gently spiced with cinnamon. I prepared it with a joint of silverside weighing 1 kg/2¼ lb; remove as much of the fat and gristle as possible but keep the beef in one neat piece. A hearty, warming winter dish, this serves four people, accompanied by mashed potatoes and celeriac or a steaming pot of polenta. This is similar to the next recipe, which comes from Naples and for which I have found no other recipes.

☞ *1 kg/2¼ lb joint of beef, well trimmed*
2 garlic cloves, peeled and slivered
4 slices Parma ham, roughly chopped
4 tbs olive oil
15 g/½ oz butter
1 onion, peeled and finely chopped
1 carrot, scrubbed and diced
1 celery stick, diced
1 bay leaf
pinch of dried thyme or 2–3 sprigs fresh thyme
salt and freshly milled black pepper
small piece of cinnamon
560 ml/1 pint full-bodied red wine
1 tbs tomato purée

With a small, sharp knife cut about 12 deep incisions into the beef. Fill them with half the garlic slivers and a chopped slice of ham.

Heat the oil and butter in a stewing pan just big enough to accommodate the beef. Fry the beef until lightly browned all over, remove and put it on a plate, then add the remaining chopped ham to the pan. Brown the ham lightly, then add the vegetables, herbs and the remaining garlic. Stir-fry until lightly coloured, season and add the cinnamon. Return the beef to the pan, together with any juices that may have collected on the plate. Pour in the wine, bring to the boil, then stir in the tomato purée. Reduce the heat, spoon some liquid and vegetables over the beef, cover the pan tightly and simmer very gently for about 4½ hours, turning and basting the beef at half-hourly intervals.

When the beef feels meltingly tender check the seasoning. Carefully remove the beef and put it on a chopping board. Remove the cinnamon, raise the heat to maximum, and reduce the liquid to a fairly thick, chocolate-coloured sauce. Slice the beef into thick rounds, arrange them on a warmed platter, pour the sauce over them and eat immediately.

Cinnamon gently spices this stracotto in a recipe the Victorians stole from the Italians. Mashed pototoes make pleasant company with this warm, hearty dish.

A NEAPOLITAN POT-ROAST

Eliza Acton's recipe for a Neapolitan stufato, in which a whole joint of beef is very slowly cooked to yield a sauce for macaroni; the beef is served after the pasta.

NEAPOLITAN STUFATO

*T*ake six pounds of the silver side of the round, and make several deep incisions in the inside, nearly through to the skin; stuff these with all kinds of savoury herbs, a good slice of lean ham, and half a small clove of garlic, all finely minced, and well mingled together; then bind and tie the meat closely round, so that the stuffing may not escape. Put four pounds of butter into a stewpan sufficiently large to contain something more than that quantity, and the beef in addition; so soon as it boils lay in the meat, let it just simmer for five or six hours, and turn it every half hour at least, that it may be equally done. Boil for twenty-five minutes three pounds of pipe maccaroni, drain it perfectly dry, and mix it with the gravy of the beef, without the butter, half a pint of very pure salad oil, and a pot of paste tomatas; mix these to amalgamation, without breaking the maccaroni; before serving up, sprinkle Parmesan cheese thickly on the maccaroni.

We insert this receipt exactly as it was given to us by a friend, at whose table the dish was served with great success to some Italian diplomatists. From our own slight experience of it we should suppose that the excellence of the beef is quite a secondary consideration, as all its juices are drawn out by the mode of cooking, and appropriated to the maccaroni, of which we must observe that three pounds would make too gigantic a dish to enter well, on ordinary occasions, into an English service. We have somewhere seen directions for making the stufato with the upper part of the sirloin, thickly larded with large, well-seasoned lardoons of bacon, and then stewed in equal parts of rich gravy, and of red and white wine.

ELIZA ACTON, *Modern Cookery for Private Families (1855)*

Cook's Tip

A piece of beef half the size may be sealed in a mixture of 25 g/1 oz butter and 2–3 tbs olive oil. Eliza Acton is right about the quantity of macaroni; just 400 g/14 oz should be perfect for an appetizer for 4–6 people, dressed with a sauce enriched by the meat juices.
To do that, wine or stock may be added to the beef, which should be tightly covered and left to simmer very gently for about 4 hours. When very tender add to the pan containing the beef 2 tbs tomato purée or the chopped contents of a small can of plum tomatoes, and simmer for about 15 minutes longer. Toss the cooked, drained pasta with some of this sauce, if desired adding some small knobs of butter, and sprinkle with Parmesan. Follow this with the beef, sliced.

Part Nine
CAKES & DESSERTS

J UDGING from their cookbooks, the Victorians evidently had a sweet tooth. Royal chef Charles Francatelli devotes an entire volume to the subject. Sweet dishes, especially in grand households, appeared not just at the conclusion of the meal, as today. Cakes and other sweet dishes such as jellies and creams were often placed on the table to be admired throughout the meal, and at formal dinners and banquets both sweet and savoury side dishes or entremets were served with the 'second' or even 'third' course, before 'dessert' which often comprised several fruits (fresh and dried), ices, filberts etc., and a fine cake such as a Savoy at centre stage. Affluent households took great pride in the presentation of their cakes and sweet puddings, and the latter were invariably shaped in highly elaborate moulds so as to look fancifully carved.

Recognizing that such elaborations are perhaps incompatible with today's tastes I have simplified the range of sweets, choosing a few typical cakes such as a Pithiviers, some fruit and a Christmas pudding by Eliza Acton, and also a lovely bread and butter pudding, delicious alcoholic syllabubs and creams, and a selection of sweet biscuits.

TRADITIONAL VICTORIAN CAKES

LEMON SPONGE CAKE

This delicious lemon sponge cake was very popular in Victorian England and was often served with a glass of sherry or Madeira.

☞ *4 eggs*
175 g/6 oz sugar
110 g/4 oz melted butter
grated rind of 1 lemon
175 g/6 oz plain flour
2 tsp baking powder

Preheat the oven to 180°C/350°F/gas mark 4. Whisk the eggs thoroughly, then slowly add the sugar, butter and lemon rind, beating thoroughly after each addition. Fold in the flour and baking powder. Grease a 20 cm/8 inch cake tin, pour in the mixture and bake for 1 hour or until the cake is golden brown and well risen; a skewer inserted into the centre should come out clean.

SEED CAKE

This traditional cake enjoyed great popularity during the nineteenth century. The quantity of caraway seeds may be varied (or indeed omitted altogether and replaced by currants), according to taste.

☞ *110 g/4 oz butter*
225 g/8 oz plain flour
3 tsp baking powder
110 g/4 oz sugar
¼ tsp ground mace
¼ tsp grated nutmeg
6–7 tsp caraway seeds
2 eggs
2–3 tbs brandy

Preheat the oven to 180°C/350°F/gas mark 4. Rub the butter into the flour and baking powder until the mixture resembles fine breadcrumbs. Add the sugar, spices and caraway seeds and mix thoroughly. Beat the eggs and add to the mixture together with the brandy. Tip into a greased 20 cm/8 inch cake tin and bake for 50 minutes or until the cake is golden brown and well risen; a skewer inserted into the centre should come out clean.

Cook's Tip

The skewer test is the sure way to check when the cakes are cooked, and can be relied upon more readily than cooking times as ovens vary, and even the atmospheric humidity makes a difference.

*Two very simple cakes that were very popular with the Victorians: a slice of lemon
sponge cake (left) was often enjoyed with a glass of sweet Madeira wine; next to it is
a cake spiced with caraway seeds and gently flavoured with brandy.*

OBSERVATIONS ON CAKES

Before beginning to make any sort of cake, have sugar beat and sifted; flour of good quality dry and sifted; the fruit stoned, or picked and washed, or rubbed in a towel; the lemon peel pared, or beat to a paste in a mortar, with a little cream; the butter, when this is used for light cakes, beaten cold to a cream; and, above all, have the eggs, yolks and whites, separately well beaten. A large tin basin answers best for this purpose, as the yolks or butter can in this be heated a little over the fire while the whisking is going on, which assists the process.

MEG DODS, *Cook and Housewife's Manual (1829)*

TRADITIONAL SPONGE CAKE

This sponge cake contains no fat or raising agents, but yet is wonderfully light by virtue of vigorous beating; grated lemon rind gives it a pleasant citrus flavour.

TO MAKE SMALL SPONGE CAKES

<u>INGREDIENTS</u> – *The weight of 5 eggs in flour, the weight of 8 in pounded loaf sugar; flavouring to taste.*

<u>MODE</u> – Let the flour be perfectly dry, and the sugar well pounded and sifted. Separate the whites from the yolks of the eggs, and beat the latter with the sugar; then whisk the whites until they become rather stiff, and mix them with the yolks, but do not stir them more than is just necessary to mingle the ingredients well together. Dredge in the flour by degrees, add the flavouring; butter the tins well, pour in the batter, sift a little sugar over the cakes, and bake them in rather a quick oven, but do not allow them to take too much colour, as they should be rather pale. Remove them from the tins before they get cold, and turn them on their faces, where let them remain until quite cold, when store them away.

ISABELLA BEETON, *Book of Household Management (1861)*

MRS BEETON'S SPONGE-CAKE

INGREDIENTS – *The weight of 8 eggs in pounded loaf sugar, the weight of 5 in flour, the rind of a lemon, 1 tablespoonful of brandy.*

MODE – Put the eggs into one side of the scale, and take the weight of 8 in pounded loaf sugar, and the weight of 5 in good dry flour. Separate the yolks from the whites of the eggs; beat the former, put them into a saucepan with the sugar, and let them remain over the fire until milk-warm, keeping them well stirred. Then put them into a basin, add the grated lemon-rind mixed with the brandy, and stir these well together, dredging in the flour very gradually. Whisk the whites of the eggs to a very stiff froth, stir them to the flour &c., and beat the cake well for $1/4$ hour. Put it into a buttered mould strewn with a little fine sifted sugar, and bake the cake in a quick oven for $1\frac{1}{2}$ hours. Care must be taken that it is put into the oven immediately, or it will not be light. The flavouring of this cake may be varied by adding a few drops of essence of almonds instead of the grated lemon-rind.

Cook's Tip

Mrs Beeton's recipe for sponge cake is entirely without fat and raising agents; yet, by vigorous beating, the cake rises perfectly and is very light and airy. Originally, this was baked in a very deep and elaborate mould but a deep-sided baking tin may be used instead. Alternatively, the mixture makes an excellent sponge sandwich cake by dividing the mixture into two shallow 20 cm/8 inch cake tins and baking at 180°C/350°F/gas mark 4 for 45 minutes or until well risen and golden brown; a skewer inserted into the centre should come out clean.

PLAIN CAKE

Mix two pounds of dry flour with four ounces of clean dripping melted in a pint of milk, three tablespoons of yeast, and two well-beaten eggs, mix well together, and set aside in a warm place to rise, then knead well and make into cakes; flour a tin, and place it in the oven in a tin; carraway-seeds or currants may be added, sugar over.

ALEXIS SOYER,
A Shilling Cookery for the People (1859)

CHILLED CAKE FOR SUMMER DAYS

PITHIVIERS CAKE

*This delicious recipe is adapted
from Francatelli's Pithiviers Cake in* The
Modern Cook *(1896 edition). It is very good
eaten at room temperature but tastes even better
chilled. Serve with cream; for four people.*

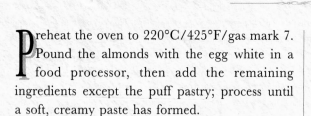

☞ *175 g / 6 oz blanched almonds*
1 egg white
75 g / 3 oz butter, at room temperature
110 g / 4 oz caster sugar
3 egg yolks
50 g / 2 oz ratafias
1 dessertspoon orange-flower water
pinch of salt
225 g / 8 oz puff pastry, thawed if frozen

Preheat the oven to 220°C/425°F/gas mark 7. Pound the almonds with the egg white in a food processor, then add the remaining ingredients except the puff pastry; process until a soft, creamy paste has formed.

Roll out half the puff pastry to fit the base of a greased shallow cake tin approximately 20 cm/8 inches in diameter. Tip in the paste, spread to within 2.5 cm/1 inch of the pastry edge, then dampen the edge with a little water. Roll out the remaining pastry and place on top of the filling, pressing the edges together. Score the top with a knife, shake some caster sugar over the cake and bake for 20 minutes or until the pastry has risen and taken on a light golden colour. Serve cold.

TO REDUCE ALMONDS TO A PASTE

Chop them a little on a large and very clean trencher, then with a paste roller, which ought to be thicker in the middle than at the ends, roll them well until no small bits are perceptible amongst them. We have found this method answer admirably; but as some of the oil is expressed from the almonds by it, and absorbed by the board, we would recommend a marble slab for them in preference, when it is at hand; and should they be intended for a sweet dish, that some pounded sugar should be strewed under them. When a board or strong trencher is used, it should be rather higher in the middle than at the sides.

ELIZA ACTON, *Modern Cookery for Private Families (1855)*

Francatelli's cold Pithiviers cake is absolutely scrumptious, with a strong flavour of almonds.

A tempting slice of Mrs Beeton's own Christmas cake is quite irresistible, and indispensable for truly old-fashioned festive eating.

MRS BEETON'S CHRISTMAS CAKE

<u>INGREDIENTS</u> – 5 teacupfuls of flour, 1 teacupful of melted butter, 1 teacupful of cream, 1 teacupful of treacle, 1 teacupful of moist sugar, 2 eggs, $\frac{1}{2}$ oz. of powdered ginger, $\frac{1}{2}$ lb. of raisins, 1 teaspoonful of carbonate of soda (baking soda), 1 tablespoonful of vinegar.

<u>MODE</u> – Make the butter sufficiently warm to melt it, but do not allow it to boil; put the flour into a basin; add to it the sugar, ginger, and raisins, which should be stoned and cut into small pieces. When these dry ingredients are thoroughly mixed, stir in the butter, cream, treacle, and well-whisked eggs, and beat the mixture for a few minutes. Dissolve the soda in the vinegar, add it to the dough, and be particular that these latter ingredients are well incorporated with the others; put the cake into a buttered mould or tin, place it in a moderate oven immediately, and bake it from $1\frac{3}{4}$ to $2\frac{1}{4}$ hours.

ISABELLA BEETON, *Book of Household Management (1861)*

ALEXIS SOYER'S PLUM PUDDING

Pick and stone half a pound of Malaga raisins, wash and dry the same quantity of currants, chop, not too fine, three-quarters of a pound of beef suet, put it in a convenient basin, with six ounces of sugar, two ounces of mixed candied peel sliced, three ounces of flour, three ditto of bread-crumbs, a little grated nutmeg, four eggs, a gill of water, or perhaps a little more, to form a nice consistence; butter a mould, put a piece of white paper over the top and round the sides, tie it in a cloth, boil for four hours in plenty of water; when done, remove the cloth, turn it out of the mould, take the paper off the sides and top, and serve with sweet sauce round; it may also be boiled in a cloth.

A DELICIOUS CHRISTMAS PUDDING

ELIZA ACTON'S CHRISTMAS PUDDING AND SAUCE

To three ounces of flour, and the same weight of fine, lightly grated bread-crumbs, add six ounces of beef kidney-suet, chopped small, six ounces of raisins weighed after they are stoned, six ounces of well-cleaned currants, four ounces of minced apples, five of sugar, two of candied orange rind, half a teaspoonful of nutmeg mixed with pounded mace, a very little salt, a small glass of brandy, and three whole eggs. Mix and beat these ingredients well together, tie them tightly in a thickly-floured cloth, and boil them for three hours and a half. We can recommend this as a remarkably light small rich pudding: it may be served with German wine, or punch sauce.

Flour, 3 oz.; bread-crumbs, 3 oz.; suet, stoned raisins, and currants, each, 6 oz.; minced apples, 4 oz.; sugar, 5 oz.; candied peel, 2 oz.; spice, ½ teaspoonful; salt, few grains; brandy, small wine-glassful; eggs, 3: 3½ hours.

A DELICIOUS GERMAN PUDDING SAUCE

*D*issolve in half a pint of sherry or of Madeira, from three to four ounces of fine sugar, but do not allow the wine to boil; stir it hot to the well-beaten yolks of six fresh eggs, and mill the sauce over a gentle fire until it is well-thickened and highly frothed; pour it over a plum, or any other kind of sweet boiled pudding, of which it much improves the appearance. Half the quantity will be sufficient for one of moderate size. We recommend the addition of a dessertspoonful of strained lemon juice to the wine.

For large pudding, sherry or Madeira, ½ pint; fine sugar, 3 to 4 oz.; yolks of eggs, 6; lemon-juice (if added), 1 dessertspoonful.

Cook's Tip

This is a truly delicious pudding, but the appearance of it is marred by flouring the cloth; tie in an unfloured cloth instead.

Re-create all the warmth and splendour of a Victorian Christmas table with the best pudding recipe, which comes from the impeccable and always reliable Eliza Acton.

Bread and butter pudding: an English dessert that cannot fail to provoke fond nostalgic memories. You will find it uncommonly delicious.

SUPERIOR BREAD AND BUTTER PUDDING

This is adapted from Eliza Acton's 'rich' recipe, although there is nothing wrong with her 'common' version, which is reproduced without modifications. This is truly a superior dessert that will appeal to anyone with a fondness for old-fashioned English puddings. Serves four.

☞ *280 ml / 10 fl oz milk*
pared rind of ½ lemon
small cinnamon stick
4 tbs single cream
50 g / 2 oz sugar
3 eggs, beaten
pinch of salt
3 tbs brandy or rum
soft butter for wiping the baking dish
5–6 slices of thinly cut white sandwich bread, buttered
50 g / 2 oz currants
25 g / 1 oz candied citrus peel

Bring the milk to the boil, add the lemon rind and cinnamon and simmer for 10 minutes. Strain and discard the lemon peel and cinnamon. Mix in the cream and sugar. Stir in the beaten eggs, salt and brandy or rum. Butter generously a baking dish approximately 17 cm/7 inches square and fit 3 layers of buttered bread, with the currants and candied peel evenly distributed between them; scatter some on the top. Pour the milk and egg mixture slowly over the bread and set aside for 2 hours to soak.

Preheat the oven to 175°C/350°F/gas mark 4; bake the pudding for 40 minutes or until golden brown and crisp on the top.

ELIZA ACTON'S COMMON BREAD AND BUTTER PUDDING

Sweeten a pint and a half of milk with four ounces of Lisbon sugar; stir it to four large well-beaten eggs, or to five small ones, grate half a nutmeg to them, and pour the mixture into a dish which holds nearly three pints, and which is filled almost to the brim with layers of bread and butter, between which three ounces of currants have been strewed. Lemon-grate, or orange-flower water can be added to this pudding instead of nutmeg, when preferred. From three quarters of an hour to an hour will bake it.

Milk, 1½ pint; Lisbon sugar, 4 oz.; eggs, 4 large, or 5 small; ½ small nutmeg; currants, 3 oz.: baked ¾ to 1 hour.

ECONOMICAL PUDDINGS

A series of Economical Puddings, which can be made either in a mould, basin, tart-dish, or cake-pan.

Well butter either, fill lightly with any of the following ingredients:- Either stale buns, muffins, crumpets, pastry, white or brown bread, sliced and buttered, the remains of sponge cakes, macaroons, ratafias, almond cake, gingerbread, biscuit of any kind, previously soaked. For a change with any of the above, you may intermix with either fresh or dried fruit, or preserves, even plums, grated cocoa-nut, &c. When your mould is full of either of the above, put in a basin a quarter teaspoonful of either ginger, a little mixed spice, or cinnamon, if handy, grated orange, lemon, or a few drops of any essence you choose; put in three eggs, which beat well, add three gills of milk for every quarter mould. When the above is well mixed, fill up nearly to the rim. It can be either baked or boiled, or put into a saucepan one-third full of water, with the lid over, and let it simmer for about one hour. Pass a knife round the inside of the basin or mould, turn out your pudding, pour over either melted butter with a little sugar, the juice of a lemon or spirit sauce.

ALEXIS SOYER, *A Shilling Cookery for the People (1859)*

MRS BEETON'S 'VERY GOOD' BAKED APPLE PUDDING

INGREDIENTS – 5 moderate-sized apples, 2 tablespoonfuls of finely chopped suet, 3 eggs, 3 tablespoonfuls of flour, 1 pint of milk, a little grated nutmeg.

MODE – Mix the flour to a smooth batter with the milk; add the eggs, which should be well whisked, and put this batter into a well-buttered pie-dish. Wipe the apples clean, but do not pare them; cut them in halves, and take out the cores; lay them in the batter, rind uppermost; shake the suet on top, over which also grate a little nutmeg; bake in a moderate oven for an hour, and cover, when served, with sifted loaf sugar. This pudding is also very good with the apples pared, sliced, and mixed with the batter.

TIME – 1 hour.

Sufficient for 5 or 6 persons.

Mrs Beeton titled her baked apple pudding 'very good':
she was right. Her recipe is for a very simple batter
pudding, with apples either cored and halved, but left
unpeeled as shown above, and mixed into the batter.
The alternative is to peel and slice the apples first.

A 'very superior whipped syllabub', extravagantly flavoured with sherry and brandy. The basic recipe for syllabub includes 'a little cinnamon' and goes on to suggest variations flavoured with, respectively, port, cider and Madeira.

SHERRY SYLLABUB

This is based on Eliza Acton's recipe for 'Very Superior Whipped Syllabub'. She observes that syllabubs are 'often made with almost equal quantities of wine and cream, but are considered less wholesome without a portion of brandy'. Serves four to six people.

☞ *1 lemon*
75 g/ 3 oz caster sugar
110 ml/ 4 fl oz dry sherry
4 tbs brandy
225 ml/ 8 fl oz double cream

Finely grate the lemon peel and strain 4 tbs of the juice into a large mixing bowl. Add the sugar, grated lemon peel, sherry and brandy. Stir until the sugar dissolves. Add the cream and beat the mixture well. Take off the froth as it rises, spoon into stemmed glasses and chill for 4 –24 hours.

Although a syllabub can be also be a hot, alcoholic milky preparation, the old-fashioned English version is always cold, and must contain cream, wine and the grated rind and juice of a lemon.

Cook's Tip

A creamier, and very delicious version can be made by continuing to beat the mixture until thick enough to hold a soft peak.

SWISS CREAM, OR TRIFLE

☞ *coarsely chopped rind of 1 lemon*
175 g/ 6 oz caster sugar
3 tbs water
4 tsp flour
¼ tsp ground cinnamon
560 ml/ 1 pint double cream
juice of 2 lemons
110 g/ 4 oz almond ratafias
25–50 g/ 1–2 oz candied citron, thinly sliced, to decorate

In a small pan mix together the lemon rind, sugar and water, bring to the boil, then reduce the heat and simmer for 5 minutes, stirring constantly. Remove from the heat and strain, discarding the lemon rind.

Mix the flour and cinnamon together with enough of the cream to form a smooth, batter-like mixture. Heat the remaining cream in a pan, add the lemon syrup and bring to the boil. Add the flour, cinnamon and cream mixture, and simmer for 4–5 minutes, stirring constantly. Remove from the heat, pour into a bowl and set aside. When completely cooled gradually mix in the lemon juice.

Take half of the ratafias and cover the bottom of a glass dish, pour in half of the cream mixture, lay the remainder of the ratafias on the top, then add the rest of the cream. Refrigerate for at least 12 hours and serve decorated with thinly sliced candied citron.

STORECUPBOARD BISCUITS

<u>INGREDIENTS</u> – One pound of flour, half a pint of treacle, two ounces of butter, half an ounce of ground ginger, a pinch of allspice, a tea-spoonful of carbonate of soda, and a pinch of salt. Mix all the above ingredients into a firm well-kneaded stiff paste, divide this into about twenty-four round balls rolled into shape like walnuts, place these upon greased baking-tins at distances of two inches apart from each other, and bake the gingerbread nuts in a rather brisk oven for about fifteen minutes.

CHARLES ELMÉ FRANCATELLI, *A Plain Cookery Book for the Working Classes (1861)*

RATAFIAS

Ratafias are good eating biscuits, and they are also an invaluable storecupboard biscuit that can be used in all manner of desserts.

☞ 2 egg whites
175 g / 6 oz whole blanched almonds
175 g / 6 oz caster sugar
butter, for greasing

Beat the egg whites until they hold a peak. Preheat the oven to 150°C/300°F/gas mark 2. Pound the almonds either in a mortar or in a food processor, together with half of the beaten egg white. Transfer to a bowl, mix in the sugar and the remaining egg white. Mix thoroughly and shape into very small, flat buttons. Bake on a greased oven tray for 40 minutes or until dry and beginning to crisp at the edges.

LEMON BISCUITS

This is an excellent old-fashioned recipe for biscuits with a lovely fresh lemon flavour.

☞ *50 g / 2 oz butter*
225 g / 8 oz plain flour
110 g / 4 oz caster sugar
grated rind of 1 lemon
1 large egg, beaten
1 dessertspoonful lemon juice

Preheat the oven to 180°C/350°F/gas mark 4. Rub the butter into the flour; add the sugar and lemon rind and mix thoroughly. Fold in the beaten egg and lemon juice. Adding more flour if necessary, knead to form a stiff dough. Turn onto a floured work surface, and roll out to a thickness of approximately 3 mm/⅛ inch. Cut and shape as required. Place in the oven on a greased baking sheet and bake for 6–10 minutes or until golden brown at the edges.

Lemon biscuits are
easy to make. The stiff dough is just
flour, butter, sugar, egg, and grated lemon
rind and juice. The biscuits bake in
just a few minutes.

Part Ten
SAVOURY PRESERVES AND PICKLES

T HE REIGN of Queen Victoria saw many dramatic social and economic changes, not least rapid urban growth and hence a huge increase in the number of households living in towns and cities. By the time Mrs Beeton completed her magnus opus, there was a vast market for her book, mainly consisting of urban housewives for whom the need to pickle their own glut of fruit and vegetables had declined.

Savoury preserves and pickles are not just excellent condiments that perk up plain meats, cold poultry, ham, and cheese, they were also required in cooking, especially in sauces. Vinegars flavoured with herbs and fruits were especially popular, and will be found both decorative and useful in sauces, relishes and vinaigrettes. What nostalgic recipe collection could be complete without such classic pickles as piccalilli, pickled baby onions, and pickled mushrooms? Pickled garlic, I admit may be more of an acquired taste. Garlic was usually present in the fruit chutneys that the Victorians acquired from India alongside the curries they loved and to which chutney is the perfect partner. I have also included slightly more exotic recipes, for example an excellent red cabbage relish, and pickled nasturtiums and chilli peppers.

Although valued as a process for making sharp-tasting relishes and condiments to enliven meats and cheeses, pickling surplus ingredients was originally indispensable for maintaining health and nutrition in the lean winter months when fresh vegetables were in very short supply. Mushrooms and onions are highly suitable for pickling.

PICKLED MUSHROOMS

Pickled mushrooms are a long-standing favourite with many European nations, especially Russia and Poland, where they have often filled in for meat and vegetables in harsh times. Wild fungi are preferred but cultivated button mushrooms at least have a good firm texture if less flavour. Serve in small quantities with ham and cold meats; their sharp taste stimulates the appetite. This will fill a medium pickling jar.

☞ *900 g/ 2 lb firm button mushrooms, wiped clean*
560 ml/ 1 pint white wine or cider vinegar
560 ml/ 1 pint water
1 tbs salt
2 bay leaves
6 cloves
1 tsp allspice berries
oil to fill the pickling jar

Trim the mushrooms but leave them whole. Put them into a large pan together with the remaining ingredients except the oil. Bring to the boil, stirring constantly, then cover and simmer for about 8 minutes. Drain, and allow the mushrooms to cool.

Meanwhile, sterilize a large glass pickling jar in boiling water or in a hot oven; if using water drain well. With a sterile spoon put the mushrooms together with their pickling spices into the jar. Fill the jar with oil, stirring to release any trapped air bubbles. There should be a generous layer of olive oil covering the mushrooms. Seal and leave for several weeks. Once opened, finish within a fortnight or so; they will only keep if you use a clean fork or spoon to remove the mushrooms.

PICKLED ONIONS

Pickled baby onions are the obvious relish for a ploughman's lunch of cheese, crusty bread and salad. Prior to pickling, the onions must first be soaked in a brine solution to soften them and draw out excess moisture.

☞ *450 g/ 1lb small pickling onions*
water
3 tbs salt
560 ml/ 1 pint spiced white wine or cider vinegar
(see page 235)

Peel the onions, taking care not to break them up. Put them in a pan, cover with water, add the salt and bring to the boil. Turn off the heat and leave them to soak for about 6 hours, then rinse and drain thoroughly.

Heat the spiced vinegar without boiling. Put the onions into a sterilized pickling jar. Pour in the vinegar, seal and store for at least 3 weeks before opening. Once opened keep in the fridge.

EXOTIC PICKLES AND CHUTNEYS

The four recipes on these pages are from Eliza Acton's Modern
Cookery for Private Families *(1855).*

CAPSICUMB CHUTNEY

*Slice transversely and very thin,
into a bowl or pan of spring water, some tender
green capsicumbs, and let them steep for an
hour or two; then drain and dress with oil,
vinegar, and salt.*

Cook's Tip

**This is a relish, not a true chutney, and has no keeping
properties. Green peppers or the large mild varieties of
chilli peppers are preferred.**

TO PICKLE NASTURTIUMS

*These should be gathered quite young, and a
portion of the buds, when very small, should be
mixed with them. Prepare a pickle by dissolving
an ounce and a half of salt in a quart of pale
vinegar, and throw in the berries as they become
fit, from day to day. They are used instead of
capers for sauce, and by some persons are
preferred to them.*

PICKLES

These are an important class of culinary preparations, and one about which the cook and notable housewife make no little bustle, and feel no small pride. Pickles are chiefly intended for a relishing accompaniment to many sorts of made-dishes and sauces, though a few of them are merely ornamental as garnishes.

MEG DODS, *Cook and Housewife's Manual (1829)*

The ancient Greeks and Romans held their pickles in high estimation. They consisted of flowers, herbs, roots, and vegetables, preserved in vinegar, and which were kept, for a long time, in cylindrical vases with wide mouths. Their cooks prepared pickles with the greatest care, and the various ingredients were macerated in oil, brine, and vinegar, with which they were often impregnated drop by drop. Meat, also, after having been cut into very small pieces, was treated in the same manner.

ISABELLA BEETON,
Book of Household Management (1861)

TO PICKLE RED CABBAGE

S trip off the outer leaves, wipe, and slice a fine sound cabbage or two extremely thin, sprinkle plenty of salt over them, and let them drain in a sieve, or on a strainer for twelve hours or more; shake or press the moisture from them; put then into clean stone jars, and cover them well with cold vinegar, in which an ounce of black pepper to the quart (ie 2 pints, of vinegar) has been boiled.

TOMATO AND OTHER CHATNIES

MAURITIAN RECEIPTS

T he composition of these favourite oriental sauces varies but little except in the ingredient which forms the basis of each. The same piquant or stimulating auxiliaries are intermingled with all of them in greater or less proportion. These are, young onions, chillies (sometimes green ginger), oil, vinegar, and salt; and occasionally a little garlic or full-grown onion, which in England might be superseded by a small portion of minced eschalot. Green peaches, mangoes, and other unripe fruits, crushed to a pulp on the stone roller...ripe bananas, tomatas roasted or raw, and also reduced to a smooth pulp; potatoes cooked and mashed; the fruit of the egg-plant boiled and reduced to a paste; fish, fresh, salted or smoked, and boiled or grilled, taken in small fragments from the bones and skin, and torn into minute shreds, or pounded, are all in their turn used in their preparation. Mingle with any one of these as much of vinegar, as will bring it to the consistence of a thick sauce. Serve it with currie, cutlets, steaks, pork, cold meat, or fish, or aught else to which it would be an acceptable accompaniment.

A POPULAR PICKLE

*Pungent, piquant piccalilli, stained bright yellow by both mustard
and turmeric; this mixed vegetable pickle, which keeps very well, dates back
to the mid-eighteenth century. The curious name is probably an amalgam
of the words 'pickle' and 'chilli'.*

*Piccalilli was a popular English Victorian pickle, traditionally
served with cold meats, cheeses etc. The vegetables may be varied according to
availability but be sure to include the peppers and cauliflower. If you can't find
ready-spiced vinegar, do make your own; it's very simple. This recipe makes
about 1 litre/ 1¾ pints of piccalilli.*

PICCALILLI

☞ *1 cucumber*
2 green peppers
12 pickling onions
¼ cauliflower
560 ml/ 1 pint water
6 tbs ground sea salt
75 g/ 3 oz green beans, coarsely chopped
1 tbs mustard powder
1 tbs turmeric
550 ml/ 1 pint spiced vinegar (see below)
3 tbs sugar

Peel the cucumber, then slice in half vertically, remove the seedy middle and discard it. Chop the flesh. Remove the peppers' caps, pith and seeds and dice the flesh. Peel the pickling onions but leave them whole. Cut the cauliflower into small chunks.

Bring the water to the boil and add the salt. Allow to cool. Throw in all the vegetables and leave them in the brine solution for at least 24 hours; this is necessary because it draws out excess moisture which otherwise would dilute the pickle. Mix the vegetables a few times to ensure that they all absorb the brine properly. Rinse and drain the vegetables well.

In an enamelled pan, make a paste with the mustard, turmeric and a little warmed spiced vinegar, stirring constantly. When the paste is smooth, add the remaining vinegar and the sugar. Mix well, bring to the boil and reduce the volume of liquid by half, stirring constantly. Add the drained vegetables, mix well, and boil for about 10 minutes. Spoon the piccalilli into hot, sterilized jars. Seal, and when they have cooled, store the jars in a cool, dark place for at least 1 month before opening, preferably longer.

KEEPING PICKLES

Nothing shows more, perhaps, the difference between a tidy thrifty housewife and a lady to whom these desirable epithets may not honestly be applied, than the appearance of their respective store-closets. The former is able, the moment anything is wanted, to put her hand on it at once; no time is lost, no vexation incurred, no dish spoilt for the want of 'just a little something,' – the latter, on the contrary, hunts all over her cupboard for the ketchup the cook requires, or the pickle the husband thinks he should like a little of with his cold roast beef or mutton-chop...One plan, then, we strenuously advise all who do not follow, to begin at once, and that is, to label all their various pickles and store sauces.

ISABELLA BEETON, *Book of Household Management (1861)*

SPICED VINEGAR

For 1 litre/1¾ pints white wine or cider vinegar you will need about 50 g/2 oz pickling spices such as: cinnamon fragments, dried sliced ginger, allspice berries, juniper berries, peppercorns, coriander seeds, green cardamom pods, whole cloves, mustard seeds, dried chillies, crumbled dried bay leaves. Heat all the ingredients in an enamelled pan; bring to a gentle simmer, stir, then remove from the heat. Allow to cool completely, then strain the liquid into a sterilized glass bottle. Seal and store in a cool, dark place until required.

PICKLES

PICKLED GARLIC

☞ *2 large whole heads garlic*
225 ml/ 8 fl oz white wine vinegar
1–2 tsp mixed pickling spices e.g. allspice, cloves,
peppercorns, coriander seeds, chillies
2 tsp sugar
2 tsp salt

Separate the garlic cloves, then bruise them very gently with a wooden mallet or rolling pin. Peel the cloves and put into a small, sterilized glass jar with a tight lid.

Stir the vinegar, sugar, salt and pickling spices over a medium-low heat until dissolved. Allow the mixture to cool, then pour it over the garlic cloves, seal, and store for several weeks before consuming. Keep refrigerated, once cooked.

Cook's Tip

Also good for pickling: gherkins; very small unripe cucumbers, beetroot, marsh samphire, elderflower buds, green beans, green walnuts, shallots, cauliflower florets.

Almost any vegetable – in this case garlic – can be preserved by pickling in hot vinegar, which kills the micro-organisms that cause fresh ingredients to decay.

FLAVOURED VINEGARS

'AN AGREEABLE ADDITION'

Flavoured vinegars are easy and fun to make as well as being useful in interesting sauces, marinades and vinaigrettes. A row of different flavoured vinegars displaying the different ingredients submerged in the bottles will embellish any kitchen.

Flavoured vinegars, which Meg Dods called 'a cheap and agreeable addition to sauces, hashes, and ragoûts' are very easy to make at home. The Garlic Vinegar is my own recipe, but the four preceding recipes are taken from Meg Dods' Cook and Housewife's Manual, *published in 1829. One quart is the equivalent of 1.1 litres/2 pints of liquid; one drachm (or dram) equals one sixteenth of an ounce.*

CHILLI VINEGAR

*I*nfuse a hundred red chillies, fresh gathered, in a quart of the best white-wine vinegar for ten days or more, shaking the bottle occasionally. A half-ounce of genuine cayenne will answer the same purpose. This makes an excellent and cheap addition to plain melted butter for fish sauce, &c.

ESCHALOT VINEGAR

*C*lean, peel and bruise four ounces of eschalots at the season when they are quite ripe without having become acrid. Steep them in a quart of the best vinegar, and strain, filter, and bottle.

CELERY OR CRESS VINEGAR

*P*ound a half-ounce of celery-seed or cress-seed, and steep it for ten days in a quart of vinegar. Strain and bottle.

TARRAGON VINEGAR

*G*ather the leaves of tarragon on a dry sunny day; pick them from the stalks, and filling up a narrow-necked stone-jar, pour the best vinegar over them till the jar is full. Let them infuse for ten days, then strain and bottle the tincture. Basil vinegar is made precisely as above. The French add cloves and lemon-rind: we admire this addition.

GARLIC VINEGAR

A very good garlic vinegar is made by inserting the bruised but unpeeled cloves of a whole head of garlic into a bottle of best aged red wine vinegar; infuse for several weeks and use sparingly.

Part Eleven

DRINKS

HE VICTORIANS drank far more alcohol than would be considered healthy under today's stringent medical guidelines. Fortified wines such as madeira, sherry, and port, and of course unfortified wine were popular tipples with the upper and middle classes, while grain spirits such as gin, and traditional ale, stout and porter were imbibed by the less affluent. The consumption of alcoholic drinks was not always delayed until the sun was over the yard-arm, and a glass of sweet wine was often offered with cake.

This final section brings together a small selection of beverages, soft and hard, including an excellent lemonade, and barley water, as well as spicy mulled wines, categorized from 'Bishop' up to 'Cardinal', and beer and champagne cups. Pray raise your glasses in a toast to enjoying Victorian food and cooking!

LEMON SOFT DRINKS

LEMON BARLEY-WATER

Notwithstanding its traditional associations with the Victorian sick-room or nursery, lemon barley water is a most refreshing drink, especially when made with plenty of lemon juice and sugar. Whether, as Eliza Acton recommends, 'a glass of calf's foot jelly added to the barley is an infinite improvement' still appeals today, is debatable. This recipe makes two pints.

☞ *50 g/2 oz pearl barley, washed*
560 ml/1 pint cold water
pared rind of 1 lemon, coarsely chopped
2.3 litres/4 pints freshly boiled water
juice of 2 lemons
3 large tbs caster sugar, or to taste

Bring the pearl barley and cold water to the boil, and simmer for 15 minutes. Strain, then add the barley and lemon rind to the freshly boiled water. Bring back to the boil, then simmer until the liquid is reduced by half. Strain, add the lemon juice and sugar and leave to cool. Check the flavourings and stir well before serving well chilled.

EXCELLENT PORTABLE LEMONADE

Rasp, with a quarter-pound of sugar, the rind of a very fine juicy lemon, reduce it to powder, and pour on it the strained juice of the fruit. Press the mixture into a jar, and when wanted for use dissolve a tablespoonful of it in a glass of water. It will keep a considerable time. If too sweet for the taste of the drinker, a very small portion of citric acid may be added when it is taken.

ELIZA ACTON, *Modern Cookery for Private Families (1855)*

Eliza Acton's 'excellent portable lemonaide' is really zestful and refreshing, just as real lemonade should be. The recipe is for a lemonade concentrate that keeps well: 1 tbs to be diluted in a glass of water.

A hot glass of spiced wine fortifies a flagging spirit like no other drink, especially during the rigours of Christmas time. Depending upon the quality and provenance of the wines used, a common mulled wine may rise through the ecclesiastical hierarchy, from Bishop, up to Cardinal.

MULLED WINE

⊷═ ◉═⊷

*H*OT SPICED WINES – A variety of these delicious potations were in use so late as the beginning of the sixteenth century...The only kind of these delicious beverages still in use, besides our common mulled wine, is Bishop, that bewitching mixture made of Burgundy oranges and spices, with sugar. When this compound is made with Bourdeaux wine, it is called simply Bishop; but, according to a German amateur, it receives the name of Cardinal when old Rhine wine is used; and even rises to the dignity of Pope when imperial Tokay is employed.

MEG DODS, *Cook and Housewife's Manual (1829)*

OXFORD RECEIPT FOR BISHOP

➤ ⟨

*M*ake several incisions in the rind of a lemon, stick cloves in these, and roast the lemon by a slow fire. Put small but equal quantities of cinnamon, cloves, mace, and allspice, with a race of ginger, into a saucepan with half a pint of water; let it boil until it is reduced by one-half. Boil one bottle of port wine, burn a portion of the spirit out of it by applying a lighted paper to the saucepan; put the roasted lemon and spice into the wine; stir it up well, and let it stand near the fire ten minutes. Rub a few knobs of sugar on the rind of a lemon, put the sugar into a bowl or jug, with the juice of half a lemon (not roasted), pour the wine into it, grate in some nutmeg, sweeten it to the taste, and serve it up with lemon and spice floating in it.'

OBS – Bishop is frequently made with a Seville orange stuck with cloves and slowly roasted, and its flavour to many tastes is infinitely finer than that of the lemon.

ELIZA ACTON, *Modern Cookery for Private Families (1855)*

REFRESHING COLD CUPS

BEER CUP

INGREDIENTS – *one quart of stout or porter, half an ounce of moist sugar, a small slice of bread toasted brown, and a small quantity of grated nutmeg and ginger. Mix these ingredients in a jug and allow the cup to steep for half an hour previously to its being drank.*

NOTE – Ale cup is made in a similar manner.

These cups are more particularly adapted for being handed round with cheese.

CYDER CUP

INGREDIENTS – *one quart of Cyder, one pint of German Seltzer-water, a small glass of Cognac, a bunch of balm, ditto of burrage, a sliced orange, one ounce of bruised sugar-candy.*

PROCESS – place the ingredients in a covered jug embedded in ice for an hour and a quarter, and then decanter the cup free from herbs, &c.

NOTE – Any other aërated water may be substituted for Seltzer, or the cup may be prepared without the addition of any water.

CLARET CUP

INGREDIENTS – *one bottle of Claret, one pint bottle of German Seltzer water, a small bunch of balm, ditto of burrage, one orange cut in slices, half a cucumber sliced thick, a liqueur-glass of Cognac, and one ounce of bruised sugar-candy.*

PROCESS – place these ingredients in a covered jug well immersed in rough ice, stir all together with a silver spoon, and when the cup has been iced for about an hour, strain or decanter it off free from the herbs, &c.

The above all appeared in Francatelli's
The Modern Cook *(1896)*

*Francatelli's beer cup is an unlikely but entirely successful and very refreshing mixture
of dark stout (or porter) steeped with sugar, toasted bread and spice.*

MINT JULEP, AN AMERICAN RECEIPT

Strip the tender leaves of mint into a tumbler, and add to them as much wine brandy, or any other spirit, as you wish to take. Put some pounded ice into a second tumbler; pour this on the mint and brandy, and continue to pour the mixture from one tumbler to the other until the whole is sufficiently impregnated with the flavour of the mint, which is extracted by the particles of the ice coming into brisk contact when changed from one vessel to the other. Now place the glass in a larger one, containing pounded ice: on taking it out of which it will be covered with frost-work.

ELIZA ACTON, *Modern Cookery for Private Families (1855)*

A splendid cup: the ingredients are champagne, sparkling water, brandy (or Curaçao), sugar and borage, mixed together with plenty of cooling, finely crushed ice.

CHAMPAGNE-CUP

*M*rs *Beeton recommends this aristocratic drink for picnics, balls, weddings and other festive occasions; they must have been jolly affairs! This is her own recipe.*

☞ *1 bottle champagne, or dry, quality sparkling wine*
280 ml/ 10 fl oz sparkling mineral water
1 liqueur-glass of brandy or Curaçao
2 tbs powdered sugar
450 g/ 1 lb finely crushed ice
some sprigs of borage or a few twists of cucumber rind

Mix everything together in a large glass jug or clean bucket.

BADMINTON CUP

INGREDIENTS – *one bottle of red Burgundy, one quart of German Seltzer-water, the rind of one orange, the juice of two, a wine-glass of Curacao, a bunch of balm, ditto of burrage, a sprig of verbina, one ounce of bruised sugar-candy, a few slices of cucumber.*

PROCESS – place these ingredients in a covered jug embedded in rough ice for about an hour previously to its being required for use, and afterwards decanter the cup free from the herbs, &c.

CHARLES ELMÉ FRANCATELLI, *The Modern Cook (1896)*

INDEX